"Winter in this starved Country"

Writings from the Valley Forge Encampment
of the Continental Army,
December 19, 1777-June 19, 1778

Volume II

Joseph Lee Boyle

HERITAGE BOOKS, INC.

Other Heritage Books by the author:

From Redcoat to Rebel: The Thomas Sullivan Journal

*Writings from the Valley Forge Encampment of the Continental Army
December 18, 1777-June 19, 1778 (Vol. 1)*

*"My Last Shift Betwixt Us & Death"
The Ephraim Blaine Letterbook, 1777-1778*

Published 2001 by

HERITAGE BOOKS, INC.
1540E Pointer Ridge Place, Bowie, Maryland 20716
1-800-398-7709
www.heritagebooks.com

ISBN 0-7884-1825-4

A Complete Catalog Listing Hundreds of Titles
On History, Genealogy, and Americana
Available Free Upon Request

CONTENTS

PREFACE

While much has been written on the Valley Forge Encampment of the Continental Army, it has not yet been the subject of a readily available scholarly history. John W. Jackson's *Valley Forge: Pinnacle of Courage* (1992), is the best currently available. John B. B. Trussell Jr., *Birthplace of an Army: A Study of the Valley Forge Encampment*, 1977, is useful, but repeats many of the undocumented, traditional stories. The three volume "Valley Forge Report" (1980-82), by Wayne Bodle and Jacqueline Thibaut, written for the National Park Service, is recommended, but it received very limited distribution.

Hundreds of letters and documents written at Valley Forge, have been published in collections such as *The Writings of George Washington* and *The Nathanael Greene Papers*. However, these represent the best remembered men of the Revolution. There are many prominent leaders, even significant general officers such at Anthony Wayne, whose papers have not been collected and published.

There are also an uncounted number of documents by lesser officers and staff functionaries, that have never been published, or have been printed long ago and are not readily available. The intent of this effort is to present a selection of these, as the second of a projected four such volumes, to allow greater understanding and appreciation of the Valley Forge Encampment. The lack of letters by private soldiers is to be regretted, but very few of these are known to exist.

The assistance of staff members at a number of institutions helped make this effort possible. These include the: Connecticut Historical Society; Connecticut State Library; Dartmouth College Library; Maryland State Archives; Massachusetts Historical Society; Massachusetts State Archives; Neilson Library of Smith College; New Jersey State Archives; New York State Historical Association; New-York Historical Society; New York Public Library; Pennsylvania Historical and Museum Commission; Prescott Memorial Library at Louisiana Tech University; Princeton University Library; Rhode Island State Archives; Rosenbach Foundation of Philadelphia; Rowan University Library; University of Virginia Library; Valley Forge National Historical Park.

INTRODUCTION

The year 1777 began well for Washington. The victories of Trenton and Princeton revived the spirits of the Patriots. For the next few months the American army encamped at Morristown, and with the Spring, gradually rebuilt itself from the losses of 1776. In June, British General Sir William Howe attempted to lure Washington into battle in the plains of New Jersey, but Washington declined combat.

In the Summer, with General John Burgoyne advancing from Canada into New York, Howe began an expedition for reasons that have never become clear. Instead of remaining in New York City and advancing up the Hudson River Valley to support Burgoyne, Howe embarked on an expedition against the American capital of Philadelphia. When Howe sailed from New York Harbor in late July with his army, American spies were well aware of the expedition, but not of its destination. Washington suspected that Philadelphia was Howe's object, and moved the bulk of his army into Pennsylvania, leaving Horatio Gates in New York to counter Burgoyne's advance.

Intending to enter the Delaware River, General Howe and his brother Admiral Richard Howe, received information that the banks of the river were heavily fortified, and that it was blocked with submerged obstructions. They then decided to sail south, enter the Chesapeake Bay, land near the head of that bay, and march to Philadelphia.

The destination of the British fleet was not known to Washington until August 22. The next day he marched the army through Philadelphia. The two forces met at the Battle of Brandywine on September 11, which was an American defeat. On October 4, Washington launched an audacious attack on the enemy then encamped at Germantown. Though ultimately defeated, even the defeat cheered the Americans, as they had routed the British in their initial assault.

After Germantown, the focus was on the Delaware River, where Forts Mifflin and Mercer, with a small American fleet, blocked the removal of the obstructions from the river. Opening the river was critical for General Howe, as he needed contact with his fleet for supply and reinforcements.

On November 2, the Continental Army moved to Whitemarsh, which was to be home for the next six weeks. After clearing the Delaware of American resistance in mid-November, General Howe marched out of Philadelphia on December 4 and faced Washington's position at Whitemarsh for three days. Finding the American position too strong to attack, Howe returned to Philadelphia on December 8.

The oncoming winter weather was becoming more and more unendurable to the poorly clad American soldiers. Permanent quarters had to be found. The army crossed the Schuylkill on December 12 and arrived at the Gulph, where it remained until December 19, when it marched into Valley Forge and began to build log huts for shelter. General Jedediah Huntington commented upon arriving at Valley Forge that "We are now setting down for the Winter in this starved Country and are to hut ourselves in the Woods—Wood is pretty plenty and so is Water....but there is Nothing else to invite us to this Place."

The six month encampment of the Continental Army at Valley Forge has long since entered the realm of American myths. Though some of the tribulations and triumphs have been exaggerated, and others ignored in popular histories, the enduring patience of the soldiers and the inspirational leadership of the "dear and good General" Washington, appear as keys to eventual victory.

Some of the stories that have become legendary are reinforced in the following letters. There are many references to the lack of shoes, blankets and clothing. General Anthony Wayne reports on December 28, 1777 that "At this inclement Season one third of our Troops are totally Destitute of either Shoes, Stockings, Shirts or Blankets, so that unless they receive an immediate supply of these Necessary Articles, Sickness, Death & Desertion will be the inevitable Consequence."

Food was in desperately short supply in December, mid-February and late May. Adjutant General Alexander Scammell lamented on February 16 about "brigades of the Soldiery sweering their pocks and in open Day declaring their Intention to go home. at the same time asserting that they could not do duty for want of food." Hundreds did indeed desert, but the wonder was that most of enlisted men stayed, not that many left.

However, references to extremely bad weather are relatively few. A review of these letters and other sources leads to the conclusion that the winter weather of 1777-1778 was actually moderate. The Army might have suffered less for food and clothes, had the temperatures been slightly colder. Mud and mire made the unpaved roads nearly impassible at times. No bridges existed over large rivers, and ferries could not bring supplies across with ice floes coming down, though frozen rivers would have allowed supplies to pass over. John Fitzgerald reported to Washington on February 16, that he was unable to cross the Susquehanna River for nine days and "when I did it was not without great difficulty & some danger."

Tardy and insufficient pay are the cause of frequent complaints. While inflation had started, it had not risen to become the problem it did by 1780. But even when the men did receive their pay, there was a often a shortage of things to buy. However, in June Peter Grubb wrote that "two Months Pay is drawn for our Division and our Men are constantly Drunk."

Some of the problems that were faced by the army, have been forgotten by all but scholars. The importance of forage for transportation animals may seem a minor concern. However the hundreds of horses in the camp needed their own rations of hay and grain, as did the animals that transported food, clothing, and other supplies into camp. Without healthy livestock to pull the wagons, the army could not receive food, clothing, and other necessities. Much of the suffering at Valley Forge was caused by the failure of the transport system to deliver available food and clothing to the camp.

Another overlooked problem that this collection of documents illustrates is that of the "country people" trading with the enemy in Philadelphia. The civilians around Philadelphia had long been accustomed to entering the city on market days to sell or trade their produce and other wares. The British encouraged this and sent out regular patrols to protect these citizens, while the Americans mounted their own patrols to stop this trade. The men at Valley Forge show more animosity towards these people, than they do towards the enemy army. Scammell bitterly comments on March 17 about "these milk & water, white livered, unsancify'd Quakers....I am apprehensive that I shall imbibe an inveterate Hatred against the whole sect, or rather against those who make a Cloak of that profession to perpetrate the blackest Villainies." Most of these people were probably not Tories, or active loyalists to the Crown, but simply trying to survive between the contending parties of the two armies.

On the other hand, the actions of the enemy army, occupying Philadelphia barely twenty miles away, are rarely remarked upon, until rumors of movement began in May, except when a skirmish occurs. Strong hatred of the British and Hessian troops is not readily apparent.

From the distance of more than two hundred years, the bickering and jealousies of some of the officers seems both trivial and all too human. All the Brigadier Generals at Valley Forge wrote to Congress, complaining that Thomas Conway, who had the least seniority, was promoted over their heads. Captains in a artillery regiment squabble over who should command the regiment "so much that General Knox ordered Col[l]. Proctor, his Lieut Col[l]. & Major to decide who was oldest, as the Senior Officer, in Brigade Orders, was to Command. They met, but did not do it;—I believe, to get clear of the trouble, recommended Cap[ts] Lee Doughty & Porter to toss up who should Command only for the present."

Another area of contention is what later came to be called the "Conway Cabal." As Washington had lost two major battles, and our capital was in enemy hands, some questions about the effectiveness of his leadership were natural. Horatio Gates, the victor of Saratoga, may have been actively intriguing with some in Congress, to have Washington replaced. Whatever the truth of this episode may have been, it has been lost in the fury and zeal of the Washington loyalists as they rallied around their chief.

There are triumphant episodes recorded. The capture of a richly laden British supply ship by General Smallwood's garrison at nearby Wilmington was a cause for elation in the dark early weeks at Valley Forge. Three weeks later, on January 20, Henry Lee successfully defended a stone house against a vastly superior enemy force, a triumph which was the talk of the camp.

One notable event that was unremarked on at the time, was the arrival of Friedrich von Steuben on February 23. But a month later Henry Beekman Livingston wrote that Steuben "is taken great notice of and is Appointed Inspector-General of the Army he is now Teaching the Most Simple Parts of the Exercise such as Position and Marching of a Soldier in a Manner Quite different from that, they have been heretofore used to, In my Oppinion More agreable to the Dictates of Reason & Common Sence than any Mode I have before seen."

Another momentous, though now largely forgotten achievement, was massive smallpox inoculation. Most people in America in the eighteenth century had no protection against this virulent disease that killed perhaps 25 percent of those who contracted it. Outbreaks of the affliction had decimated armies for centuries. There were as many as four thousand men inoculated at the camp in the early months, and many more in the Spring with the arrival of new recruits. Very few of these men died, despite poor accommodations, limited hygiene, and inferior nutrition.

The greatest elation of all occurred with the news that France and the United States had signed Treaties of Alliance and Commerce. This prompted a huge celebration and *a Feu de Joie* on May 6, and in conjunction with persistent rumors that the enemy was about to evacuate Philadelphia without a fight, greatly cheered the soldiers. As George Fleming noted on May 14 "Our Men are in good health & high spirits. Joy sparkles in the Eyes of our whole Army."

Some camp rumors appear in these documents. In January William Gifford comments that Colonels Ogden and Martin from New Jersey had resigned. He was not correct, and both men served until much later in the war. Commonplace concerns abound. Adjutant General Scammell was "suffering for want of a good Leather Ink pot, and a good Penn-Knife" and asks an officer to send into enemy held Philadelphia and have one of each brought out to him.

Whatever their position or rank, the men at Valley Forge deserve our admiration and respect, for their steadfast determination and accomplishments in the face of numerous hardships.

Birdsboro, Pennsylvania   Joseph Lee Boyle

EDITORIAL PROCEDURE

The documents in this collection are arranged chronologically for the six month period of the Valley Forge Encampment. When more than one document of the same date appears, they are arranged alphabetically according to writer.

Letters are introduced by the names of the addresser and addressee. The dateline falls just below the heading, though the original document may have it at the bottom. The complimentary close is brought up flush with the last paragraph and the closing signature has been omitted. A descriptive note at the foot of each entry shows the location of the document presented, and identifies the writer and recipient the first time each individual appears.

These documents present a literal translation with spelling, punctuation and grammar remaining as they are found in the original, as are the typographical errors in the printed documents. Each writer's abbreviations and contractions are also preserved as they are found in the manuscripts.

Capital letters follow the text of the originals, although it is often a guess whether a letter is a capital or not. Brackets indicate questionable or illegible letters and words. *Sic* is used very sparingly as it would quickly detract from the text, given the numerous variants of spelling and oddities of expression.

Many of the writers of these documents failed to conclude their sentences with periods, and used commas, colons, or semicolons instead, if anything at all. Dashes were frequently used by some, such as Jedediah Huntington, and these have been duplicated.

Crossed out material has been omitted. Margin notes are shown as postscripts, except where obviously keyed to the body of the document.

The index includes the names of all persons. However place names are selected, depending on relevance and frequency. Casual references to New York, for example, have been omitted.

Jedediah Huntington to Jeremiah Wadsworth

My Dear Sir,   Camp Valley Forge 21st Decr. 1777
     I was in Time favoured with your valuable Letter of the 30th with its precious Contents and yesterday brought me yours of the 12th. of this Month.
     The Spirit did not accompany the letter. I enquired of the Bearer who accounts for its not coming as he says he was to call but did not—
     I think I have explained to you the Affair of Red Bank in some former Letter, a Committee of General Officers was sent to view the Circumstances of the Fort upon the first Apprehension of the Enemys Intentions of landing at Billings Port, who were of Opinion it would be expedient to evacuate it whenever the Enemy appeared near it in Force sufficient to invest the Place as it was impossible it could hold out a siege of two Day, unless Succours should arrive in season to oblige to Beseigers to raise the Seige—my Brigade with three others were ordered for that Purpose but not in Season—it might have been earlier ordered if we had been better agreed as to the Importance of the Place—some People think there is Nothing but their own state worth defending but this is <u>entre vous</u>
     We are now setting down for the Winter in this starved Country and are to hut ourselves in the Woods—Wood is pretty plenty and so is Water for we are close upon Schuylkill, but there is Nothing else to invite us to this Place—Congress mean I suppose that we should watch the Enemy and keep them in the City—but I will project for them suppose they should leave Philad^a. with only a sufficient Garrison say 3000 Men who will be able to defend the City as well as three Times the Number and the Rest of them go to NYork which they may do in a few Days, then who will defend Connecticut that has more subsistance in One Town than I think there is in any County about here—suppose a Feint should be made at New London to draw down the Militia there and then a Scene or two like that of Danbury should be played in the western Part of the state.
     I intended to have scribbled a little more but the Bearer is ready to set out so conclude with that I am—Dear sir your sincere Friend & hble servant

Source: Jeremiah Wadsworth Papers: Correspondence, Connecticut Historical Society. Huntington was a Brigadier General from Connecticut. Congress appointed Wadsworth Commissary General of Purchases on April 9, 1778.

Enoch Poor to Henry Laurens

Camp Valley Forge 22^{d} Decr. 1777

M^{r}. Israel Evans has performed as Chaplain to five Continental Regiments in my Brigade from the first of September Last to this Time, to the General Satisfaction of both Officers and men, Therefore do Recommend that he be Appointed as Such to my Brigade—

Source: RG 360, Papers of the Continental Congress, M 247, Roll 100, i78, v18, p159, National Archives. Poor was a Brigadier General from New Hampshire. Laurens was President of the Continental Congress. Congress appointed Evans to be Chaplain of Poor's Brigade on January 5, 1778.

Henry Beekman Livingston to Robert R. Livingston

Valley Forge 24 Decr. 1777

I have so much to write of more Importance that I can say but little of our situation here—let it suffice for the present to tell you that we have retreated to within six miles of Brandywine on the West side of School Kill with our front towards Philadelphia and are now building huts for our winter quarters without nails, or tools so that I suppose we may possibly render ourselves very comfortable by the time the winter is over—Our troops are in general almost naked and very often in a starving condition, through the mismanagement of our commissaries who are treading in the paths of our Quarter-masters and Forrage-masters who have already starved our horses. Burgoyne's Army was not worse served with forrage when in their greatest distress. The enemy are rolling in the fat of the land, having played the soldier sufficiently to secure them the best of Quarters. All my men except 18 are unfit for duty for want of shoes stockings and shirts, breeches and coats: hats they can do without though it's disagreable, and to add to this miserable tale we are becoming exceedingly lousy; I am not myself exempted from this misfortune the few shirts I had with me are quite worn out what I shall do for a new stock I am at a loss to determine.

Source: Bancroft Transcripts, Manuscript Department, New York Public Library.
Henry Beekman Livingston was Colonel of the Fourth New York Regiment. Robert
was his brother in New York.

Tench Tilghman to Lord Stirling

My Lord   Head Quarters Valley Forge 25th. Decr. 1777
        Yours of 6 OClock yesterday came to hand in the Night. We
detained the Messenger till this morning to see whether any thing
further would turn up. A parcel of Waggons were sent off to you. His
Excellency seems to be of opinion with you that while the Enemy
remain in their present position nothing further can be done than is
done, but he desires you will give him instant intelligence of the least
Motion.
        I wish we could put them in mind tomorrow Morning of what
happened this time twelvemonth. I am my Lord Y^{r}. most ob^{t}. Servt.

Source: John Reed Collection, Valley Forge National Historical Park.
Lord Stirling was a Major General from New Jersey, whose name was William
Alexander. He claimed the title of Earl of Stirling, and was universally called Lord
Stirling by Congress and his fellow officers. In the last paragraph, Tilghman is referring
to the American's victory at Trenton.

Benjamin Flower to Thomas Wharton Jr.

Hon^{d}. Sir,   Camp Great Valley, 26th Decem^{r}, 1777.
        I have accidentally mett Thos. Urie Esqr. at Camp, who was
going to Allen Town with an Order on Mr. Stiles for all the Stores in his
possession & Care, either the propperty of the Continent or of this State
without specifying either Quality or Quantity—
        As M^{r}: Stiles has in his Care all the Ordnance Stores left at Allen
Town for the use of the Army, and Mr. Urie only wanting Rifles, a
small quantity of Powder & Flints, I presumed your Excellency did not
mean that he was to receive a larger quantity of Mil^{y} Stores than was
sufficient for the present emergency—I therefore have Orderd the Com^{y}
of Ord. Stores at Lebanon (where the greatest part of our Stores are
movd to,) to deliver to M^{r}. Urie or his Order—three hundred pounds of
powder and two thousand Flints—and have wrote to the Com^{y} of Stores
at Allen Town, to procure all the Rifles there and send them on to

Lancaster to M^r. Henry agreable to the request of M^r. Urie. As his Horse had given out and himself fatigued, I have undertaken the Business for him. I shall leave Camp in a day or two, when your Excellancy may rest assured that every part of the Business in my power shall be duly attended to.

I am well aware of the propriety of this State being supplies with Mil^y. Stores, from those of the Continent as all the Stores of this State have at different times been procured for the use of the Continental Army, and since our removal from Phil: all our Stores have got mix'd in such a Manner that a distinction became very difficult and I believe impossible. Therefore, all supplies necessary for the Defence of the State, ought to be had of the Continent Stores, at least whilst the War is carried on in it, in order to accomplish which it will be necessary to procure an Order from the Hon^l. the Board of War for the United States for such Mil^y. Stores as you may want from time to time, which Order I shall Chearfully and punctually attend to, as far as lies in my power.

In future our Stores will be kept at Lebanon and Carlisle, to which places you'l please to direct
I have the Honour to be Your Excellancys most Obed Hum^l Servt.

Source: RG 27, Reel 13, Pennsylvania Historical and Museum Commission.
Flower was Commissary General of Military Stores. Wharton was President of the Supreme Executive Council of Pennsylvania, then in Lancaster. He was in effect the governor of the state.

John Laurens to Henry E. Lutterloh

December 28, 1777, Head Quarters
His Excellency desires me to inform you, that, from seeing the Mill in our neighborhood unemployed, he has his doubts with respect to the activity of those which are more remote. He requires you to exert yourself as much as possible, in procuring from them all without delay a sufficient quantity of Plank for covering the new Bridge to be thrown over Schuylkill. His Excellency desires likewise, that you will send one of your Department immediately to visit the old Bridge and make an expert report to him of its present Condition.

Source: George Washington Papers, Reel 46, Library of Congress.
Laurens was an Aide-de-Camp to Washington. Lutterloh was Deputy Quartermaster General, and had been acting as head of the department for several months.

Henry Knox to Sebastian Bauman

Dear Sir,   Park 28th December 1777
    I received your Letter of yesterday, respecting a promise I made you early in the Campaign to appoint or recommend you to his Excellency to be appointed Major of Col^o. Lambs Battalion of Artillery. I well remember it, and did according recommend you to his Excellency for the Commission to whom the matter was perfectly agreable, but Colonel Lamb to whom I wrote upon the Subject objected, because in the appointment of the officers of six Companies with which he was indulged there was an older Captain in the Continental Line than you Viz^t. a Capt. Mott. Altho' Colonel Lamb was permitted to nominate his Lieu^t Col^o and the greater part of the officers of six Companies, yet he well knew that he was not to be permitted to appoint his Major—
    I always intended you for the Major of that Battalion and when I arrang'd the different Companies into Battalions, I purposely threw yours into Col^o Lambs as the oldest Captain, that your promotion might be regular and without the least difficulty, not dreaming that Col^o Lamb had appointed an older Captain than yourself.—I should not by any means thought it improper to have made you Major under these circumstances as Capt Mott had come into a new Line, but it was a case of delicacy. Col^o Lamb who is a good officer and to whom the Continent in my opinion is indebted for his services declar'd that he should take your appointment as a tacit desire for him to resign, and intimated that he should do it accordingly—upon this I thought it would be for the good of the Service to suspend the matter untill I had seen Col^o Lamb when I intended to have endevor'd to Convince him of the propriety of your being appointed—
    I think myself bound by the common principles of Justice to say that in my opinion there is no officer in the Corps who can claim promotion upon juster grounds than yourself—an assiduity in and knowledge of your profession, have justly entitled you to the esteem of all the general officers under whom you have serv'd—from these considerations I think the Service would suffer a loss by your resignation and I wish you therefore to endevor to content yourself untill I see Colonel Lamb, tho indeed I cannot promise any thing from the interview. but as there are now four Battalions of Artillery, (including one coming from Virginia) and your one of the oldest

Captains among them your promotion will be certain. The Officers are to be put on a respectable establishment, I should therefore be unhappy that you would by resigning lose the fruits of your labour and beg you still to continue in the Service—You may rely upon this that while at the head of the Artillery I shall make your promotion my care, whilst consistent with the good of the Service—If you should wish to see your family, it be granted to you as you have other Capable officers with whom your Company may be intrusted. I am Dear sir with Hble Servant

Source: Sebastian Bauman Papers, Manuscript Department, New-York Historical Society. Knox was Brigadier General of the Artillery. Bauman was a Captain in the Second Artillery Regiment.

Anthony Wayne to Thomas Wharton Jr.

Dear Sir,   Mount Joy, 28th Dec[r], 1777
I was favoured with yours of the 12th Instant, but the enemy being then out prevented me from acknowledging it sooner.

I can't help expressing both surprise and concern at the Councils directing the Clothing Collected in this State, into the hands of the Clothier General, especially after being Informed that the other States were Collecting Clothing for the use of their own Troops; Clothing for the Eastern Troops has actually arrived, they are now comfortable whilst ours are perishing.

His Excellency has also Informed me that Gov. Henry of Virginia, has ordered on Clothing for the Troops of that State which he expects every hour.

Thus Sir, whilst others States are exerting every power (under a Resolve of Congress) to provide for their own Troops only, you are following the generous course of providing for the whole, this Sir, is being generous out of time. Its an old adage, that a man ought to be just before he can be permitted to be generous, the case applies in full force here. Supply the immediate wants of your own Troops first, and then give scope to your Generosity.

Enclosed is an estimate of the cost of 650 Suits of Uniform which Mr. Zantzinger has provided for the Troops of this State; he is in great want of Money, I wish you to assist him to the cash he wants and take some Effectual Method to Cloth the Troops in the best, speediest and neatest manner possible.

Least you should be under a Deception with regard to the mode in which the Clothing in the hands of the Clothier General is Distributed, I am to inform you that they are delivered in proportion to their wants, (or in plain English) to the number of men in each Regiment throughout the army.

Judge then how far inadequate our proportion must be to out wants, whilst the Troops from the other States have an equal Division in addition to their other Supplies.

At this inclement Season one third of our Troops are totally Destitute of either Shoes, Stockings, Shirts or Blankets, so that unless they receive an immediate supply of these Necessary Articles, Sickness, Death & Desertion will be the inevitable Consequence.

I am your Excellencies most Ob^t Hum. Ser't

P.S. I have directed Mr. Zantzinger to call on you for money, I wish you to order the Clothier Genl. to estimate the price of Clothing, which agreeable to a Resolve of Congress is to be in proportion to the pay of the officers and men, the State to be at the cost of the Surplus.

Source: John Reed Collection, Valley Forge National Historical Park. Wayne was a Brigadier General from Pennsylvania. He was then acting as a division commander.

Jedediah Huntington to Jabez Huntington

Dear Sir,   Camp Valley Forge 29 Decr. 1777

As the Opportunity is so good by Lieut Avery I can't help embracing it, thou' I scarcely find Time by Reason of One Business and another to write just now—hope to have more Leisure in a few Days when I shall put Miss Moore in Mind of me by a Letter—

Please to give my Love to her and to Mama &C &C—

the Men from Connecticut engaged for Eight Months set out this day in a Body under the Conduct of some Officers for Home—their Arms are to be lodged at Fishkills—their Blankets should be returned to the state or the Value of them taken out of the Bounty that is due to them from the State—

Perhaps a good Opportunity will present of sending me a Horse before M^r. Ellis returns and perhaps he will choose to ride a Horse of his own, in that Case he can't bring mine—

Congress have appointed General Conway (who resigned the other Day in a pet) Major General & Inspector General of the Army, this Appointment gives universal Umbrage to the General Officers of the Army as much to those who are still above him as to those under him —he was a Major only in the Irish Brigade in France with the Rank of Colonel—has had great Experience or rather has been long in Service—his Genius is not more than middling—his Intrigue is infinite and his Ambition unbounded, I don't think any thing will satisfy him short of the chief Command—his Appointment is an Insult to the Understanding and Sensibility of the general Officers of the Army—the promotion of Adj: Gen[l]. Wilkinson gives great Disgust, there are no less than thirty Colonels who have signed their Resignations in Consequence of it, Congress could not have fallen upon any Measures so dangerous to the Army and more pleasing to the Enemy who well know how much Delicacy All Armies have in this Point—& I can't help believing the honest and well meaning Part of Congress have been imposed upon and duped by a Cabal which I am confident is in and about them—why may we not suspect as much when we know that Galloway—Allen &C are gone to the Enemy—a Regard to the good of our Country and a Love to our dear and good General (who some wish to have out of the Way) prevents our resenting the Indignity in the most resentfull Manner, we might with great Propriety tell Congress that we consider the late Promotions as an ingenious Intimation that they wish we would Leave the Service—but lest the Cause should suffer by such a Step we shall perhaps do no more than remonstrate—

I hope Colonel Trumbull will accept his Appointment at the Board of War—please to give my Love to him and tell him he must accept for a thousand Reasons which I could tell him of—

the General seems determined to keep us all about him the Winter so that I despair of seeing Norwich which adds much to the Disagreable Things here—but I will try to do the best I can—and hope for better Times—I wish Col Trumbull might see this Letter—please to give my Love to Miss Moore—I am wearied & got the head Ach, if I should attempt to write her it would be such a poor dull performance as would not be worth the reading I am your affectionate son

Please give my Love to Col Williams and tell him I never received his Letter of the 29 Nov[r]. till this very day—I wish him to See what I say as to the late Appointments—Congress are intirely mistaken as to the Merits of General Conway—I should suspect myself of Selfishness was not my Prospects of Advancement so far distant and besides did not I find the Matter as offensive to those who are no ways affected but from a Regard to the Advantage Peace and Honour of the Army and the Salvation of the Country—

Source: Connecticut Historical Society. Jabez was the Jedediah's father. The promotions of Thomas Conway and James Wilkinson to the ranks of Major and Brigadier General, respectively, created a great deal of resentment among Colonels and Brigadiers who were more senior, and felt they had been bypassed for no good reason.

Richard Platt to Alexander McDougall

Dear General   Camp Valley Forge Decr. 29th. 1777
      The 19th. Instant our Army moved from the Gulph Mills this Side of Schuylkill to where it now lies—It remains no longer a Doubt where our winter Quarters shall be, being already determined that the Army shall hut it—the Dimensions of the Huts are 16 feet by 14 & one is to be allowed to every twelve nonCommissioned Officers & Privates, one to the Comm^d. Officers of two Companies, one to the Field & one to the Staff Officers of each Reg^t. arranged in the order of a regular Encampment—The Sides and Ends of the Huts are to be made with logs & the Roofs of Split Slabs—And in Order to encourage the Soldiers & excite their Ambition, his Excellency has promis'd a Reward of 12 Dollars to the Party in each Reg^t. which finishes their Hut in the quickest & most Workmanlike Manner—Were it not for the scarcity of Axes & other necessary Tools most of the Troops would have been comfortably covered by this Time—But our misfortune in those Respects together with some bad weather & scarcity of Wood has prevented the Business from being completed—I have not seen what Proficiency the Front Line has made; but assure you that your Division is more forward than any other in the second Line & in a fair Way of being very comfortably covered in the course of Week at farthest from this Time—Some Huts which are already finish'd are very dry and vastly preferable to many Houses I've seen—At present the Troops remain in Tents—
      General Howe with the main Body of his Army moved out of Philadelphia the 23rd. or 24th Instant with a view of collecting Forage— In Consequence of which a Capt. & 40 men from every Brigade in the Army were sent our seperately & independant of each other—They were ordered to harrass the Enemy as much as possible & skirmish with

them wherever they found them—Besides Lord Stirlings Division & the Riffle Corps were detach'd but never were engaged that I heard off—

The Enemy surpriz'd at finding Parties on almost every Side & attack'd at every Move they made, kept very compact & made no Detachments—They came out no farther than Darby & retired to Philadelphia the night of 27th. & I believe without accomplishing their proposed Plan in a very great Degree—Some Prisoners were sent in by our Parties.—

I suppose you'll think it almost incredible, when I tell you that for three or four Days since the Army has been on this Side of Schuylkill, the greater Part of it was without Meat of any Kind—In fact our Necessity was such that Parties from every Reg^t. were sent out to take live stock & provisions of any kind wherever it was to be found—But the Difficulty is now remedied & provisions are regularly served to the Troops—

Yesterday arrived in Camp the Superintendant General to the American Army, with the Rank of Major Genl. vizt. Genl. Conway who has been hanging about Congress, till he has got Promotion—I cannot say what his Powers are, but from his Title one would imagine, very ample—This I have from Genl Forman who is late from Congress—The Brigadiers I learn are much offended at his Promotion & determined to resent it in a spirited Manner, but not to leave the Army at any Rate—

A French ship has lately arrived at Portsmouth with 48 Pieces of brass Cannon, 19 nine Inch Mortars & a quantity of military Stores—

Genl Sullivan has undertaken the Direction of a Bridge to be built over Schuylkill at Fatland Ford, near about the Center of the Army & which is almost ready to raise—

On my Way to Camp I wrote a Note to M^r. Sheetz desiring him to come to Camp & I would pay him—He came accordingly some Days after & I thought proper to borrow the Money to pay him not having received your Pay as the Pay Master Genl. had not arrived—I mention this supposing it will give your mind some satisfaction in that Respect—As soon as I receive your Pay shall send it & inclose Scheetz's Receipt & Account—

Genl Parsons I hear has been on Long Island again, but has not accomplish'd his Plan—

Col^o. Saml Webb, Col^o. Eli, 2 Majors & 40 men of Webb's Reg^t. were taken on their way going over.

This Day the eight Month's Men belonging to your Division march'd for Fish Kill where they are to be discharged—

I am Dr Genl with respects to M^rs. McDougall & Stephen, your most Obed^t. Servt.
Margin Note: Inclos'd is a Letter for Stephen which I found in Camp—

Source: Rosenbach Foundation, Philadelphia, Pennsylvania. Platt was a Major and Aide-de-Camp to McDougall. He gives a good description of the problems then facing the Continental Army. McDougall, a Major General from New York, was then at Morristown, New Jersey.

George Weedon to George Washington

Dear Sir   Valley Forge Decr. 29th 1777
    On considering what appears most proper to adopt in this Army, for a permanent system in future promotions, regulations, and arrangements; I would beg leave to suggest the following hints—
    First.—All continental commissions below the rank of Brigadier to issue by the Commander in Chief upon the following general rule; except where extraordinary merit takes place; to which retrospect should ever be had; (to wit)—Regimental promotions by regular succession to the rank of Captains inclusively. All promotions in the line of Field officers to go by the line of state to which they belong. This has been some time observed and gives general satisfaction.
    Each state having right to a certain number of General officers, Congress should make it an invariable rule, from this general arrangement of the Army, to promote the eldest colonel in the state, when vacancies fall in the line of General officers belonging to said state, provided his former conduct was compatible with the officer & Gentleman. They holding at the same time the priviledge of rejecting if found otherwise. Promotions for certain political reasons should be clearly ascertained before given. The system of presidence would be regular and just.
    In arranging the army I would propose the Troops now raised by the different states, to be thrown into Battalions of eight Companies, each Company to Consist of one Captain, two Lieutenants, one Ensign, four serjeant, one Drum, one Fife, and sixty four rank and file. This number of privates makes four divisions of sixteen men each, which is full sufficient for a young subaltern to command; It being found from experience, that troops well officered always render most certain

service. This number is also convenient in laying off for marching by sub divisions or platoons. The Battalion should be Commanded by one Lieutenant Colonel Commandant, who should receive the same pay and exercise the same authority as the present Colonels do. This would give an opportunity for exchange in case of Captivity which at present cannot be effected with the British Army, they having no such officers as Colonels in America.

On this principle, each Battalion would consist as follows—one L^t. Col^o. Commandant, one L^t. Col^o, one Maj^r. 8 Captains, 16 $Lieu^{ts}$, 8 Ensigns, 32 serjeants, 8 Drums, 8 Fifes, & 512 Rank & file.

The supernumerary officers if any, by this arrangement, should be sent to their different states recruiting, or to receive and discipline Drafts, till such time as vacancies happen in their Regiment or line, when they should be called to fill them agreeable to their several Ranks.

The different states should be immediately directed to fall on ways and means for raising their full number of Battalions to compleat any deficiency this arrangement may leave, agreable to their first Quota, alloted by Congress, which Battalions should be under the above regulations.

The Army should be immediately put on the American establishment for life; upon similar principles with the British Army: officers Commissions made transferable under certain regulations and prices for each rank: New Commissions fill'd on Parchment, to issue with the seal of the united states affix'd. Permission to purchase in or sell out, left to the discretion of the Commander in Chief. No person to be allow'd to purchase in at first higher than an Ensigncy: nor to purchase over the heads of Lieutenants till they refuse to buy: and so with the other ranks to a Regiment, and no purchases to be allow'd higher. This would be a sure means of always having good and frugal officers.

All Titles in the staff of the army (unless they hold Commissions in the line) to be totally abolish'd and annihilated as a nuisance to refin'd notions of Rank. It has already prov'd fatal to the service and frequent experiments discover errors. No established uniform to be allow'd any person whatsoever, but the officers and soldiers of the Army.

One regular system of duty to be immediately adopted for the whole line. Trifling as the small duty's of a Camp or Garrison may appear, they are in their Consequences very essential, and require strict attention and uniformity. Relieving Guards, posting sentinals, going the rounds, receiving the officers of the day, receiving the Commander in Chief, reporting occurency's, &c^a. &c^a. should be done in a regular Military manner: One set of plain Manoeuvres fix'd on, and no others practis'd, one Manuel to be performed throughout the whole Continental line: The whole to be Compris'd in a small book and each officer furnish'd with one at his own expence, that he may know his duty, and not plead ignorance for Neglecting it.

I should be for allowing the Q^r M^r. General to hold rank in the line. His Commission as an officer would stimulate him to his other duties.

The Forage M^r. Genl. should hold neither rank or title, but should be a steady industruous man; honest in Character, and remarkable for sobriety.

The Waggon M^r. General should be some noted person, well acquainted with the nature of Teams and Waggons who has chiefly subsisted by his Industry that way.

One half of the present staff belonging to this army are nothing more than sinecures without the least benefit to the publick. They impoverish the Magazines; Strip the Country and debauch the army. For having nothing to do, and holding rank at the same time, are the only Gentlemen of pleasure and gallantry. Great reformation is wanting in these Departments.

In fixing on a proper uniform, respect should be had to the scarcity of articles. I would propose a short Coat, cuff'd and Cap'd only with different colours—a short Waistcoat without skirts, a small round Hatt black leather, or hair stock, overalls summer and Winter. In summer of Linning; In Winter of Wooling. One Certain time of the year should be fix'd on for Cloathing the whole Army: I mean with such necessaries as are allowed them by the publick. These should be served out about the first of December, and should consist of the following articles—Viz. 1 Coat, 1 Vest, 1 p^r. Leather Breeches, 1 p^r Woolen overalls. 2 pr. Linnen D^o., 2 shirts, 1 Hatt, 1 p^r. stockings, 2 p^r. shoes, and 1 stock.

If any of these hints meets your Excellencies approbation I shall be made happy.

I am With due regard Your Excellencys most ob^t. serv^t

Source: George Washington Papers, Roll 46, Library of Congress. Weedon was a Brigadier General from Virginia. Washington had requested suggestions on the reforms and improvements needed in the Army and its support services.

Henry E. Lutterloh to Ozias Bingham and Deputy Quarter Master Generals in New England

Head Quarters, Jan^ry 1st. 1778
The Bearer Ozias Bingham is Authorised to raise and Engage some Waggoners as Drivers to Inlist for three Years certain, he is to promise each Man the Bounty Money of Twenty Dollars, and during his Time of the Service, Sixteen Dollars pay p^r Month, Continental Currency. The Men so engaged for three Years certain, must Sign their Engagement before a Justice of the Peace, And then from that Day their Pay Commences, also their Daily Rations, in want of them M^r. Bingham is to pay for their daily Provisions in the best and Cheapest Manner, Also every Waggoner so intitled is to have like a Soldier his Cloathing, whenever the Regiment or Brigade drawes, and receives Cloathing to which he is Allotted to Drive.
P. S. You must also from Time to Time send off the Men to the Army, as the keeping them there only increases the Expences. You must also give me often Reports how you go on—

To, The Deputy Q^r. Master Gen^ls. in New England—
In case M^r. Ozias Bingham should want any Money for paying to the Waggoners, which he has an Order to Inlist for the Continental Service, You will be pleased to lett the Men be brought to you, and After they have taken their Oath, to Advance them the Bounty Money, with Twenty Dollars p^r Man, And your Orders for the Advanced Money shall be Honoured with Repayment—

Gentlemen
    If M^r. Bingham Apply's for Money to pay for Horses which he has bought upon my Order, I request you will be pleased to Advance him, The Money; by sending off the Horses to my Order, and I will repay you the Advanced Money—

Source: Jeremiah Wadsworth Papers: Correspondence, Connecticut Historical Society.

James Mitchell Varnum to Nicholas Cooke

Sir—   Camp Valley Forge Janry 3ᵈ. 1778
     By Colᵒ. Comstock you will receive this. I have to acknowledge your kind favor by the Hands of Colᵒ. Barton. I am much indebted to you, for the Kindness express'd in the Contents.
     Colᵒ. Comstock will fully explain the Nature of his Errand, & give you every Intelligence of our Situation. Colᵒ. Greene, and some other Officers will follow in a short Time, by whom I shall write you more fully upon the State of the Rhode Island Troops, and the Necessity of increasing their Numbers to the proper Establishment. I have the Honor of being, with great Respect, your very obdᵗ. & very humble Servᵗ.—

Source: Letters to the Governor: vol. 9, p. 115. Rhode Island State Archives.
Varnum was a Brigadier General from Rhode Island. Cooke was Governor of that state.

Robert Ballard to Timothy Pickering

                         Camp 6ᵗʰ of January 1778
Dear Sir   Tuesday evening 4 Oclock
     I have been out of Camp since Saturday which prevented my receiving your favor of the 4ᵗʰ Insᵗ. till just now. I observe Mʳ. Hughes has been pressing you for an enquiry into his conduct respecting what I had heard by the Carolina Officer & had spoken of as hearing at Genˡ Muhlenbergs Quarters. I shall be obliged if you'll inform Mʳ. Hughes once more that I do not charge him of any ungentlemanlike conduct at Norfolk or at any other place, that what I had said, was, with an intent to serve him; but as he is so very fond of any enquiry I have no objection to his having forty if he chooses it, but that the writing which he has of Mʳ Beals will not avail him anything, as I will not admit that in evidence, and as the Gentlemen who I Intend to make use of as Witnesses (& who can clear me of any intended Slaunder to Mʳ. Hughes Character,) are gone to Virginia. I must object to Mʳ. Hughes having an enquiry if my name is to be made use of, till those Gentⁿ. return, they are Genˡ Muhlenberg & Lieuᵗ Col Green.
     In order to satisfy Mʳ. Hughes, I intend to look for this Carlᵃ. Gentⁿ. to morrow, & will call on you, at which time I can better

inform you of my intentions. I am sorry to give you so much trouble & beg leave to return you my thanks for your favors. I am very respectfully Dr Sir, Your mo. Obed^t Servt.

Source: Timothy Pickering Papers, Massachusetts Historical Society.
Ballard was Lieutenant Colonel of the First Virginia Regiment. Pickering was Adjutant General of Washington's army. He left the Army later January for a new post as a member of the Board of War.

Lachlan McIntosh, Henry Knox, William Maxwell, Enoch Poor, George Weedon, Jedediah Huntington, Charles Scott, John Paterson, and James Mitchell Varnum to Congress

The Confidence we feel in the Candor and Integrity of Congress induces us to make this Representation.—A full Persuasion that they injure not thro' Design, but are willing to redress every real Grievance, makes us happy in their Power.—As the Fathers of a numerous, free and virtuous People, they endeavor the Happiness of all:—As the great Source of military Authority from whence flow the Existence, the Support and the Laws of the Army, they delight in it's Discipline, Subordination and Perseverance:—With these they expect to triumph over lawless Domination and wellcome the returning Sweets of Peace and Plenty.—There is no Difficulty so great but their Troops are willing to encounter:—There is no Danger so iminent but they despise in Comparison to the Freedom of America.—They have fought!—Victories & Defeats have attended their Efforts—They are acquainted with both, and determine to profit by the past.—

The Oppressions of Britain first caused an Army of Americans, and the Ideas of violated Priveleges are Still recent in their Minds. But while they feel the Rights of Citizens, they deeply imbibe the Sentiment of Soldiers—A Sense of Honor and Desire of Fame, excited by a laudable Ambition, teach them to glory in their Profession.—The Officers were citizens: Public Virtue urged them to the Field:—They accepted such Commissions as Congress were pleased to bestow:—They well knew that their Situation must expose them to the Sacrifice of Property, domestic Ease and probably Life itself.—But the brilliant Scenes which lay before them controul'd every other Consideration.

They consider'd the general Calamities of War as ever attendant upon the Struggles of a brave People ingaged in the cause of Freedom; Which added to a Thirst of Glory Stimulated them to endure the more rugged Conditions of the Camp.—Conscious that Ambition alone could lull for a series of time the native Feelings of the human Heart, They expected the Reward of military Toils.— Promotions in a regular Line as Circumstances might offer—they esteemed the necessary appendages of a well regulated Army; the Basis of Subordination and the Life of Discipline, Without which the Spirit of Enterprize is lost, the martial Ardor Chill'd and the Sensibility of the Officers wounded in the tenderst Part.—There have been many Instances in which Congress have deviated from these principles.—

Our Silence upon the Occasion has arisen from an inviolable Attachment to the great Cause of our Country.

But while we esteem our Obligations to the Public superior to every other Tie, we cannot stifle the Feelings of human Nature.— Unhappy as it is, Necessity obligates us, to mention the late Promotion of Brigadier General Conway. We have commanded him in the Field and are totally unacquainted with any superior Act of Merit which could intitle him to rise above us.—Thro' the severities of three Campaigns we have struggled with almost insurmountable Difficulties, to deserve the Approbation of our Countrymen.

To be disgrac'd by their Representatives, the Great Council of the States, without the least Imputation of Demerit, fills us as Citizens, with the deepest Concern; As Soldiers and Men of Honor we doubly feel the Indignity.—"Honor will judge of it's own Injuries"— & no Power on Earth can render us callous to all Impressions.—We wish not to depart from our Duty, but in Pursuance thereof chuse rather to point out, than resent our Grievances:—In doing which we doubt not, but we shall receive the Approbation and Relief of Congress.—

We have the Honor Sir, of being with great Respect, your very obedient humble servants—

Source: RG 93, M 247, Papers of the Continental Congress, Roll 179, item 162, volume 2, pp. 276-79, National Archives.
The nine signers were Brigadier Generals. They were protesting the fact that Thomas Conway, the least senior Brigadier, had been promoted to the rank of Major General the month before. Note on the documents states it was read in Congress on January 19, and "Ordered to lie on the table." In order words, Congress ignored this protest.

John Crane to Eleazer Wheelock

Valey Freeind[s]18 Milds From Philadelphia
Reverend Sir   January 6 1778
I am now in General Washentons Camp imployd as a Surgeon
in Co^{ll}. Vose regiment General Glovers brigade Massachusets forces
= we have had no Battle of consequence as yet Sence I have ben with
y^e Armey I am this minet informed Some of our people took a ship or
two in y^e Delaway By reason of there being blocked up with the ise
they Say of great Consequence with a large quantity of clothing on
board: perhaps you would be glad to know in what maner we are
Dispos'd of in y^e wintr campain we are Situeated on a Large hill of
woods in little Log huts y^e campe is a bout 5 milds in length and half
a mild wide a most grand perade
his Excelency G: Washenton is much Beloved by all rankes = I am in
grate hopes some way will Turn up where in I may Be of Servis to our
College: I am appointed By our feald officer to wait on y^e Congress
on Business Some Business of y^e regement:
pleas to Deliver enclose to my wife pray be a Father to her = I aske an
interest in your prayers for me & Famely in my absence: pray will
you condesent to correspond with me—I am Reverend Sir with great
respect your Very humble Servant
N:B: I am obliged to write under greate disadvantages ask your
pardon—

Source: Mss. #778105, Dartmouth College Library.
Crane was a Surgeon in the First Massachusetts Regiment. Wheelock was President
of Dartmouth College.

Elias Boudinot to Thomas Wharton Jr.

D^r. Sir   Camp Jany. 7th. 1778
I yesterday discharged Charles Dingey from the Provost, on
his giving me three Suretors in £1000, for his appearance at Lancaster
within Ten Days—I promised to return the Bond, on your Certificate
of his being properly conducted to you, but as I am bound for Jersey
think it best to enclose it to you, which you can give up when you
please—The Charge ag^t. him here is, his attempting to go into
Philadelphia, his acknowledging himself a Subject of King George

the third, and his refusing to take the Oaths or Affirmation of Allegiance to the State, or to give his Parole that he would not do us any Injury—

I have no News, but that our old Friend Ric[hie] is at last discharged, which I have informed M^r. Searle of—

Am with Compliments to M^{rs}. Wharton Dr Sir Your very Hble Serv.

Source :John Reed Collection, Valley Forge National Historical Park.
Boudinot was Commissary General of Prisoners and had just been elected a Delegate to the Continental Congress.

Jedediah Huntington to Jabez Huntington

Hon^d. Sir,   Valley Forge 7 Jany 1778

I suppose this will find you at Court, I doubt not every Member will be convinced of the Importance of making the most vigorous Efforts, Connecticut has exerted itself beyond most, if not any of her Sister States—I wish I could come Home to give the Reasons why she must do more than her Part—my greatest Dependance is upon Virginia and New England—South Carolina is too far off from the Scene of Action—this State is large enou, but there are so many Quakers in it, but little is to be expected—As much Provision as possible, should be salted in NEngland and Secured for the Army—whether they like the Comisary or not, if we get such Numbers into the field as we hope we shall, we must look for large Supplies from NEngland, especially from Connecticut—there are not, and I fear will not be, any considerable Magazines in these Parts—we live from Hand to Mouth and are like to do So, for all any thing I see—A Committee from Congress and the Board of War have been expected here a long Time to lay the Plans for next Campaign is not it astonishing they are not yet in, every Thing may be lost by Delay— Arguments the most forcible and irresistible urge us to take the Feild, with an adequate Force, early in the Season—we ought not to relax in the least, from the Prospect of a War between England & France, or from the Belief that the former is unable, or will decline, continuing her Hostilities tis as much as her Credit or even her Existance is worth to discontinue them, before she is absolutely obliged to do it, she can but fall then, as I think she must—

When the State pauses upon its Superabundant Exertions and Expence, they must console themselves with the Reflection that the Seat of War is without their Borders—an Army, even a friendly one, if any can be called so, are a dreadful Scourge to any People—you cannot concieve what Devastation and Distress mark their Steps—

The Drafts or their Substitutes who were engaged to the first of January will have their pay Continue to a reasonable Time for them to get Home—

Please to give my Sincerest Respects to the Governor, Col. Williams &c. your affectionate Son

Source: John Reed Collection, Valley Forge National Historical Park.

Henry Knox to Ebenezer Stevens

Dear Sir,   Camp Great Valley, 7th Jany 1778.

I received a few days ago your Letter of the 17th. Novr. last enclosing the Return of the Cannon and Stores which you have at Albany—a most Noble Park indeed, and highly honourable to the Army which acquired them—I hope they will long remain in the hands of the Americans.

I am sorry that you complain of not having received any Letters from me in the course of the campaign, and that you say you have written often to me. I am sure I have answered all the Letters received from you; but to have given you any particular directions without being acquainted with circumstances was impossible.—I have a high esteem for you, which is founded on the universal character given you, of a brave, and vigilant Officer, and have ever considered it as a credit to Claim connection with you.

My sentiments of an Independent Corps of Artillery are widely different from yours—I cannot conceive of an Independent Corps being in any well regulated Army whatever. An Army consisting of independent Corps would Soon prove the impropriety of the measure—I know not how far you have considered yourselves independent, nor upon what grounds. Your three Companies were raised by Massachusetts and considered by that State as a part of Colonel Crane's Battalion, and by them and me arranged as such. Whether you have received powers from Congress, or other superior authority, I know not.

I wish to do every thing for you in my power consistent with the general good of the service.

The honorable Congress will soon take such methods as to completely fill up the Several Battalions of Artillery. Massachusetts will fill up the three Companies with you and the nine with Col. Crane to 60 men each.

Capt. Lieutenant Johnson with the other Officers and men here belonging to your three Companies have been very unhappy at their situation their accounts being unsettled and they at such a distance as rendered a settlement impossible. I ha[ve] therefore ordered them to join you at Albany, and it is his Excellency's orders that Lieu^t. Hall and the men with him return as soon as possible to the Companies they belong to now at Head Quarters.

I know not what operations may be in view to the Northward to render so much Artillery necessary at Albany. If there should be no enterprize which would require it a considerable part will be ordered here for the service of the Grand Army.

I shall set out for Boston in two days in order to make preparations and arrangements for the next Campaign.—I wish you to write me and if you may require any service in my power I shall be happy to execute it.

Please to present my regards to the Officers with you, and believe that it will ever afford me a sensible pleasure to promote the Interests consistent with the good of the service.

I am Dear Sir Your must ObDt & Humble Servant

Source: *Magazine of American History* 2, no. 10 (October 1878); 616-17.
Ebenezer Stevens was Major of Stevens' Provisional Artillery Battalion. He was then at Albany, New York.

Jedediah Huntington to Jonathan Trumbull

Sir,   Camp, Valley Forge January 9, 1778
        One of our Deputy Comisaries of Prisoners was in Philadelphia a few days ago. M^r. Balfour an Aide de Camp, asked him if *the controversy* could not be settled. Several officers expressed themselves in a stile that imported their despair of subjugating the country. The necessity of bringing a formidable force into the field early in the spring glares in every point of view, and I am sure has

appeared to you and many others. Comparing present things with the past there is but little to do; the outlines of the army are drawn, we have a considerable body of veteran troops with many experienced officers. If we may believe what the conduct of Gen[l] Howe spoke at White Marsh, *he* does not despise our strength. We want our corps filled; the artillery and light horse should not be neglected; the light horse are the most usefull part of the army.

I hope the situation of our military affairs will not be seen through any false mirrour. They (N. England must not depend too much upon their sister States; neither confine themselves to the lines of proportion and equality. One grand effort will prevent, perhaps, several campaigns. How they will be rewarded for their great exertions I pretend not to say, but that they will be, I fully believe, nay, so greatly partial is a kind Providence to them, especially to Connecticut, I think they owe every thing for the superior and distinguished blessings they enjoy. I wish you all divine assistance and support under your unceasing care and labours for the publick liberty & happiness, & remain with unfeigned affection & esteem, Your Excellency's most obedient servant.

Source: "The Trumbull Papers," *Collections of the Massachusetts Historical Society*, 7th ser. (1902) 2: 211-12. Trumbull was Governor of Connecticut.

John Chaloner to John Ladd Howell

Sir   Camp Valley Forge Jan[y]. 12th. 1778
        You will imedeately proceed with the party Orderd out under the Command of Col[o]. Stuart, & do your utmost endeavours to purchase all the Flour, Fatt Beef & Pork that you may find in the Counties of Philadelphia & Bucks—or such part thereof as Col[o]. Stuart may Judge to be in danger of the Enemy, & subject to be lost by their excursions—
        You must give receipts for all Fatt Cattle estimating the weight, & Rate them from 9[d] to 12[d] p[er] lb. exclusive of the 5th Quarter according to Quality, & the same Prices for Pork or Swine—for good Wheat the Owners delivering it at such Mills as Col[o]. Stuart may direct weighing 60[lb] p[er] Bushel 12/—Flour 35/.   You must collect of each any every of these Articles all such as may appear to you to be over & above, what may be necessary for the Consumption of their Families & forward the same to Head Quarters: as fast & as expeditious as

convenience and Circumstances will permit—Persons having any of the above Articles to spare & unwilling to part with them must be compelled, Col°. Stuart will furnish Necessary Assistance for this purpose—You must be exceedingly careful not to distress persons retired from the City & also to prevent the Soldiery from committing insults on the Inhabitants or want only injuring them in their Property— Yours &c

Source: Stewart Mss. 358.8, Rowan University Library.
Chaloner was the Assistant Commissary of Purchases posted with Washington's Army. Howell was also an Assistant Commissary of Purchases, and was later stationed at Middletown, Delaware.

Henry E. Lutterloh to John Laurens

Dr Col.   Janry 15 1778
    I have inlisters out Now to get Drivers & have allready engaged 46 Men to Serve during the War. It has been my Constand Speaking about the Absolute Necessity to have drivers for a longer Term, as all our Continentel horses have been Spoiled thro' the Solders, besids No Regularity could be expected from Men which could leave the Teams & wait under the protection of their officers. it also Weakened the Army. This has been my Argument wrote Many Times—but I never Could get a positive order to go to the Expence of Inlisting—besids I waited to Know wherefrom I should get the Cloathing which I absolutely Must have to Keep the Men in Order. I have Now Send my Inlisters out, upon my own accord Knowing it must be So, but if I am not furnished with a Resolutiuon and Agreeing to those Terms of Cloathing I shall be in a pretty Situation, as I do not like to promise the poor fellows a Supply which the will not get. It is Customary abroad that all our Drivers are Anuually Cloathed & then the Waggon Masters are obliged to luck [sic] after their Cloathing as a Captain after his Soldiers—as Soon as My Men come In I will allways Discharge the present Soldier Drivers—& I am

Source: George Washington Papers, Roll 46, Library of Congress.
The use of soldiers as teamsters for the Quartermaster Department was a source of frustration to Washington, as it took them out of the ranks of fighting men. However, it was difficult to hire teamsters on the terms allowed by Congress.

Clement Biddle to Timothy Matlack

Sir   Moorhall Jan: 18, 1778.
This day I received your favour of 12th. inst. relative to the
Cloths & Shalloons belonging to M[r]. Joseph Carson—some time ago I
received an Order from His Excellency, General Washington to
Collect Clothing or Articles necessary to make them for the Army &
to give an order for such as I collected on the Clothier General or to
pay for them at reasonable rates—some time in December the General
having received information that M[r]. Carson had a quantity of leather
Breeches & some Cloth I was orderd to Easton to procure the same—
on my arrival there I met M[r]. Carson who delivered me about 1100
pair Leather Breeches, which he expressed great willingness to
furnish the Army with & he inform'd that besides a bale of Cloth
which was there & delivered me he would supply Ten or Eleven
Bales more of Cloth & Shalloons which he had offered to Mease &
Caldwell but they thought the prizes [sic] too high or the Clothes too
good for the Army—I knew the want of them & that the Generals
order to me were too urgent to loose so valuable a prize—M[r]. Carson
not only informed me where they were but soon after gave an order
on M[r]. Burr in whose possession they were in the great Swamp to
deliver them to my Order—I told him he should be allow'd a just
price for them & he Assured me the Bill he delivered was much Less
than he could have for them but I Could not even form a comparative
Judgement of the prices as I neither saw the Cloths except One bale
unopend & was unacquainted with the prices current—I can only say
that M[r]. Carson was very willing to part with them to the Army &
informed where they were when they could not otherwise be found—
that he insisted on the prices charged in his Bill as reasonable—I was
bound to take them without fixing the price—his readiness to deliver
them I conceive entitles him to the full value such Cloths sold for at
that Time—

The removal of the Sick prevented me taking the Cloths from
the swamp til I sent an express to Col[o]. Hooper to send a number of
waggons to remove them to Lancaster when I received for answer that
the Lieutenant of the County had seized them for this state, which I
conceived to be the most proper Application that could be made of them
& of course did no more on the Occasion—

You will please to communicate this to Council from sir Your
mo. obed[t] Serv[t],

I lately received a Letter from Capt Biddle of the Randolph Frigate in which he informs me your Son was well & much respected for his good behaviour.

Source: RG 27, Roll 13, frames 548-50, Pennsylvania Historical and Museum Commission. Biddle was Commissary General of Forage, responsible for providing feed for the army's work animals. Matlack was Secretary of the Supreme Executive Council of Pennsylvania. Moore Hall is a Georgian style house which still stands, two miles west of Valley Forge.

Israel Shreve to Mary Shreve

Dear Polley,   Camp at Valey Forge January 19th 1778
I now send two Letters at once I Suppose this will be the most Exceptable I here send one Hundred Dollars,—out of which sum I Desire you to pay Major Eyres forty two Dollars and make out with the Remainder as well as you can, untill I Come to see you which Shall be as soon as I Can, tomorrow morning I shall set out for Jersey once more on Command for Cloathing for our Brigade. I Shall Stay but a few Days there, the Pay master M^r: Peck has not yet arived. I Have Collected this sum, and shall Do all in my power to supply you with money sufficient to make you Comfortable &ca.—
As for News I have but Little, General Lee has arived this Day from his Long Exile. Hurry the Taylor with my Coat that I may have it when I come to Reading I will pay the Taylor when I Git it.—
        I am your Constant Loveing Husband
P: S: My Respects to M^rs: Sullivan and Peggey—my self, John, and Docters Howell and Elmer is well.
This I Send by Capt: Beecker

Source: Shreve Papers, Department of Special Collections, Manuscripts and Archives, Prescott Memorial Library, Louisiana Tech University.
Shreve was Colonel of the Second New Jersey Regiment. Either this letter is misdated or Shreve was misinformed, as General Charles Lee, who had been captured by the British in 1776, was not paroled until April 1778.

John Crane to Eleazer Wheelock

Reverend Sir   January 1778
I am not willing to wearey your patience with So little consequence you are the Best medem of Conveyence of letters to my wife: this I hope will ansur as an apolegy = as to anything publick I Do not know of anything turn^d. up to Vew: I informed you in my other letter of a Valuable prise fell into our hands Several of y^e inemys ships Blew aground in y^e Dallewa with a great quantity of clothing &c the preticulares you have or will have in the papers our armey is Very healthy. I have the care of one Brigade and no one has died out of it Sence I have had the Care of it: in this Days return there is but Eight Subjects for the hospitle our Bregade Consistes of a bout 13 hundered now on ye ground I am informed this Southeren armey consists of about 20 thousand: it is allmost two incredible to Express what a Sight of provision & forege is Consum^d in this Campe there is not less then two thousand Horses in this Camp: all the field officers & Surg[eons] are alowed to keep Each of them one on publick Forrege as well as maney others: provision of all kind are Exeding Dear the articual of potatoes is 2 Dollars pr Bushell & other things Equivelent—The State of Penselvaney where the army now is By fare the Major part Torys or them Sort of cretures call nuters it a bounds with them Proud [fan]iceal quakers. who Say that for Consence sake they cannot shed human blood: yet Do all the Mischief they can behind the Curtain they are abomaintaed & rejected by both armeys: everything reletive to the movments of the army is keept Exeding internace if I knew of aney movments to be made, I have no rite to mention it by letter or any other way: While I am Writing this intelegence is arived to camp of a Scurmish hapened Last night betwene 6 of our Light horse & upward of one hundred of the inemys horse that came out to take this Little party = the action hapened in the Night our people Secured them Selves in a Stoon hous & Defended them Selve: the Inemy retreated Left 2 kiled 4 wounded so bad they could not take them a way: pray be So good as to write me: if you could Supert a letter as I have Directed my wife it will reach me and only I am reverend Sir Your Verey humble Servt
NB I tould you our armey Consested of about 20 thous^d but there is near one quarter part on furlow: the other quarter have no shoes to their feet at this inclement season of the year the provisions we draw consist of beaf & flower only.

Source: Mss. 778140, Dartmouth College Library.
The skirmish Crane refers to happened on January 20, 1778, which dates this letter to
January 21. Henry Lee, the father of Robert E. Lee, held a stone house against a
vastly superior British raiding force. This action stone house was a major morale
boost for the army and is further described in several of the following letters.

George Fleming to Sebastian Bauman

Dear Sir,   Grand Camp, 21st Jany. 1778
    I had the unbounded Pleasure of receiving yesterday Forenoon
your much esteemed Favor of the 13th Instant, pr M^r. Morris, which
informs me of your safe arrival and Families Health.—

I observe how Busily you employed your Time, but that was
not unexpected, as I know from experience that you always are
Infatigable.

I have received Octobers Pay—paid the Captains, also your
Officers, and let the Men have theirs, retaining the overplus in my
Hands, which I shall take care of according to your desire, 'till I see
you. Capt. Doughty has Novem^{rs}. Pay Rolls, and is to leave them with
Col^l. Commandant Crane this Day—Our's he has had a considerable
Time.—

I note your directions to leave Serj^t. Danl. Cockran out of
January's Rolls. A day or two ago I listed a Matross, a well Sized
good Man; He was a Waggoner to the Artificers: which keeps our
Number good. Capt. Doughty, as usual, Swears upon it, & I laugh.

I procured of Genl. Knox, a few days after you left this Place,
a Furlough for Luke Norestrant for about six or seven Weeks, which
was the longest Space I could get him; he sett out in a day or two after
for Morris Town, and was to deliver a Letter of mine to you: I much
fear he has got sick on the road, as I have heard nothing of him since.
I let him have October's Pay and Advanced him November's.—

George Garland incessantly plagues me, for the Furlough you
promised his Uncle Barcley you would get him to see his Wife. I
recollect you promised it, and if I dont much mistake told me to get it.
I have evaded applying for it yet, as I found so much trouble in
getting Lukes; but shall shortly ask Col^l. Crane for it—not doubting I
will meet with your approbation, whether you told me or not, in
consequence of your promise to Mr. Barcley.

Your Chest of Blankets I will send you by the very first
oppertunity.

I shall present your Compliments to Col^ls. Crane & Proctor, also to the other Officers in the Park. Major Shaw is gone to Boston with General Knox. All Col^l. Cranes Captains, except Capt. Serjeant, are gone to Boston.

Captain Doughty Commands the Eight Companies; There has been a good deal of disputing between him and Captain Porter for the Command—so much that General Knox ordered Col^l. Proctor, his Lieut Col^l. & Major to decide who was oldest, as the Senior Officer, in Brigade Orders, was to Command. They met, but did not do it;—I believe, to get clear of the trouble, recommended Cap^ts Lee, Doughty & Porter to toss up who should Command only for the present. They have not tossed up, nor does Capt. Lee incline to it. As Capt. Lee has leave of Absence for six Weeks, Capt. Porter consents to Capt. Doughty's giving any Orders for the good of the Service.—

Yesterday Morning early we were Alarmed & Mann'd our Guns expecting an Attack. The occasion of it was two Hundred British Light Horse took a circuitous March to take the Intrepit Capt. Lee of our Light Dragoons & his Party; they surrounded him in his Quarters, which was defended by him, Major Jemison, who accidentelly happened to be there, Lieut. Lindsey, a Corporal & three Men against the Enemy—drove them off, killing two & wounding four, which they took Prisoners, without loosing a Man that was in the House, or getting a Person wounded except Lieut. Lindsey. They had the Generals Thanks for their Valour &c in yesterdays Orders.

We have been in our House some time; its exceeding comfortable. The Country People bring in Provisions fast. His Excellency is about establishing a proper Market, or proper Markets.—

The Company continue much as when you went away— always ready to go through Fire and Water. The Men are very contented & comfortable in their Houses, but have not quite all Shoes yet—Quantities are expected every day. The Method of Exchanging raw Hides for Shoes answers surprizingly; in a little while there will be by far more Shoes than necessary for our whole Army.

The Ax I shall not forget.—

just learn that Capt Lees Brother in Law came [   ] [Ph]ilad^a. yesterday, and says, notwithstanding the [   ] Genl. Washington has gave to the Inhabitants to come out for small quantities of Flour, they are in a Starving condition.

Please to present my respectful Compliments to M^rs. Bauman & Family. I remain, Dear Sir, with Messrs. Hows & Nestils Compliments in conjunction with my own, Your most Obed^t. Hum. Servt.

Source: Sebastian Bauman Papers, Manuscript Department, The New-York Historical Society. Fleming was a Captain Lieutenant in the Second Artillery Regiment.

Henry Beekman Livingston to George Washington

Sir,   Camp Valley Forge 22^d: Jan^y: 1778
          May it please your Excellency
                    Could I at any Time have embraced an Opinion prevalent in the Army, That the Indignity with which an Officer is treated, when by an Act of the Legislature or Ruling Power he is superseeded in Rank renders him justifiable in withdrawing himself from the Service of his Country, I should long since have followed the Example of Many others and resigned my Commission. But tho' I am Clearly of Opinion those ought to be held in a despicable Light, who, can wraped up in Luxury & Ease remain Quietly at Home on this Pretext, While Tyrany is extending ruin And devestation around them; And cannot help rendering the little Efforts in my Power as a Duty not to be dispensed with on any Account While the dark Cloud of Adversity still Continues to threaten my Friends and Country with Impending Ruin: Yet at that same Time the Promotions Over my Head in an Arrangement made by the State of New York and the Late extraordinary Rise of a Gentleman in the Northern Department are matters of real Concern to me when I reflect that it May one Day fall to my Lott to be commanded by those Formerly my Inferiors in Rank and not entitled to this superiority by their past Experience or the possession of any extraordinary Military Merit: To avoid a Mortification so grievous as well as Prompted by passions that in these distressing Times Influence many I am Induced humbly to request of Your Excellency the Command of a Partisan Corps as the only remedy to the Evils I dread, with leave to put in practice every Strategem in my Power for Anoying the Enemy by embraceing all Opportunities of surprizing, harassing, and distressing them and to avoid any Inconvenience that Drafting men from other Corps might be attended with I would desire to include only my Own Regiment at present, with leave to add to them by Inlistment four

Hundred Horsemen to act in Conjunction. The Cavalry to consist of eight Troops, Each to have one Captain, one first Lieu^{nt}. one second a Quarter Master two Serjeants and forty eight Horsemen Including a Trumpeter and Farrier The Horse to be under the same regulation with respect to pay, Cloathing, Horses Arms &c. as other Regiments of Horse now in Service The respectable Light in which these Corps have formerly been placed and the recent Services of Col^{o}: Morgans which tho composed only of Infantry have been found of Great Utility I am persuaded will rather dispose Your Excellency (Should You disapprove this Plan) rather to pardon a mistaken Zeal than Blame my presumtion—

I Am Sir with the greatest Respect Your Excellencies Most Ob^{t} Humble Servant

Source: George Washington Papers, Roll 46, Library of Congress.
Livingston did not the "Partisan Corps" he asked for, but did not resign until 1779.

William Gifford to Benjamin Holme

D^{r}. Col^{o}.   Camp at Valley Forge Jany. 24 1778

I shou'd have wrote you before now, had it not been for our Expectations of going to Jersey to Winter Quarters,—but I fancy we may give up our notions of Jersey & Content ourselves in these Wigwams this winter,—We are encamped about Twenty Miles from Philad^{a}. at a place called the valley Forge, along the Schuylkill. The Army is divided into Two lines front & Rear, besides Corps de Reserve, and possess very Commanding & defensible ground, we are fortifying the Camp as fast as possible, tho' we are under no apprehensions of a visit from the Enemy, (Tho' such a report is current in Camp) but I am very sensible they know better things, if they shou'd come I trust in God we shall be able to give them a warm reception, perhaps a total defeat, We have a large Army in every respect fit for Action; Tho' some are very bare for Clothes, I wish with all my heart our State wou'd make better provision for our Brigade, respecting Clothing & other necessaries than they do, if they had any Idea of the hardships we have & do undergo, they Certainly wou'd do more us, [sic] than they do, I assure you Sir we have had a very Severe Campaign of it, Since we came in this State,—

our Men are in huts 16 by 18, covered with Oak Shingles, and now are pretty Comfortable—since they have got to live in 'em, we lay in Tents until the 20 instant; an instance of the kind hardly ever known in any Country whatever, but what can't brave Americans endure, Nobly fighting for the rights of their injured Country.—

I Congratulate you on the arrival of 8 Ships from France under Convoy of a 40 Gun Frigate at a Port in Maryland, their Lading is uncertain but Supposed to have necessaries for the Army.—

As you are acquainted with Captain Lee of the Horse, I will mention Some thing that happened [to] him a few Nights past. On the 19 ins^t. about day break, 200 of the enemies Horse surrounded his quarters, with an intent to take him by Surprise,—but Captain Lee's vigilance baffled their designs by industriously posting his men in their Quarters, although he had not a sufficient number to allow one for each Window, he Obliged them disgracefully to retreat after Repeated & fruitless attempts to force their way into the House, leaving Two killed and four wounded, their Wounded they took off.—

We received no other damage than a Small patrole of Horse, Consisting of four fell unfortunatele in their hands, as they were returning from their post, & Lieu^t. Lindsay Slightly wounded in the wrist.—The Commander in Chief has returned Capt. Lee, his Officers & Soldiers of his Troop, his warmest thanks in General orders for their good Conduct and Superior bravery.—Captain Lee had in the House but a Corporal & 4 privates.—

Perhaps you will think I have forgot you, in not writing to you oftner than I do, I must confess I have been careless about writing, but I assure you Sir it's owing to my not having time or Paper to write on, I shou'd be ungrateful to the last Degree, if ever I shou'd forget you my best friend.—I wrote you immediately after the Action of Short Hills, and likewise after the Battle of Brandywine, in the first I mentioned the Person at Morris-Town, which I think wou'd be agreeable in every respect.—

When I shall have the pleasure of Seeing you is uncertain—if you have a Safe opportunity send me Warm[est] breeches & Stockings [ ] great care of the Linen as that article is very dear and hard to be purchased, Colonels Ogden and Martin, with a number of other inferior officers of this Brigade have Resigned.—

I Shall be very fond of hearing from you when an opportunity offers, my best respects to Col^o. Jno. Holme Capt. Sayre, Jenny,

Geo[rge] and your family & remain D^r. Col^o. your assured friend to serve you if in me lay.—

Source: Revolutionary Era Documents, #50, New Jersey Historical Society.
Gifford was a Captain in the Third New Jersey Regiment. Holme was a Colonel in the New Jersey Militia.

Richard Platt to Alexander McDougall

Dear General   Camp Valley Forge Jan^ry 24th. 1778
Yours of the 17th. Instant came safe to Hand—Previous to it I had sent a Letter to Stephen with Dunnivan's Pay to the 1st. of Sep^r. & Justice's Pay for 4 Months by Doctor Turner of Col^o. Green's Reg^t. with Directions to leave it at Col^o. Remsen's Morristown—Whenever I draw more Money for Dunnivan I shall forward it to you—I should have forwarded your Money long ago, had I drawn it; but there has not been any in Camp since my arrival. I should likewise have sent you frequent Camp News, but trusting you were at Morris Town & as Officers from your Division were daily going home by that Rout; suppos'd they would call on you, as they all promis'd, & their Furloughs coming thro my Hands I enjoined it upon them—

I have the Satisfaction to give you the following Intelligence, which I had from Genl Huntington who had it from a Member of Congress viz.

That Congress having ratifyed the Convention on their Part between Genl Gates & Burgoyne, have resolved not to suffer Genl Burgoyne & his Army to embark, till it shall be ratifyed by the Court of Great Britain—

That Congress in Consequence of a Remonstrance from the Colonels of the Northern Army have appointed Brigadier Wilkinson, Secretary to the Board of Warr—

That Genl. Spencer has resigned & his Resignation accepted by Congress—

I have likewise the Pleasure to inform you of a most gallant Defence made by Capt. Lee of the light Dragoons & of the Victory he obtained over a Body of the Enemy's Dragoons in Number about 200 who having been apprized of his Situation cross'd Schuylkill & by a very circuitous Rout thro Woods & Fields surrounded the House where he lay—his Party consisted of a Major Jemison (who accidentally fell in with him the Night before) himself, his Lieu^t. a Corp^l. & 4 Dragoons, which he placed at the Windows—The Enemy made frequent Attempts to force the House, but were repulsed in every Attempt & obliged to retire with the Loss of 2 Kill'd & four wounded which were left behind, their Commanding Officer was also wounded in the Thigh, but carried off—Our Loss none killed & only L^t. Lindsey slightly wounded in the Hand—This I think among many, is a convincing proof of what determined Valour can do—

The Genl. has given him & his party his warmest Thanks in Genl. Orders—

Our Army is now very comfortably covered, I wish I could say as well clad, but the poor Soldiers of our Army are almost naked, your Division is the best clad of any in the Army & furnishes more than 1/4 of the Duty in Camp for that Reason—There is at least 5 or 600 £'s worth of Clothing in our Division which has been sent on from Connecticut & which the Troops do not want—They have drawn their Allowance & are allowed to buy what they want besides—And notwithstanding this there is more than they know what to do with—

Genl. Howe has threatened to pay us a Visit when our Huts were compleated, but has not yet made his Appearance—

We are fortifying our Camp by Redoubts in front of the first & second Lines—

Genl. Sullivan has the Direction of a Bridge which is building over Schuylkill, & it is almost completed—

The Brigadiers have thrown in a Remonstrance to Congress respecting Genl. Conway's Promotion but have not received any Answer yet—His Excellency has never yet publish'd his Appointment in Genl. Orders, & I believe never will—Genl Conway is greatly disappointed & chagrined, indeed to such a Degree that he has taken his Quarters at a Distance from Camp & scarcely ever comes in it—

This Day the Genl. Officers have a Meeting in order to establish a Market in Camp, the Measure 'tis thought will succeed—

Congress have at length resolved to allow the Officers the full price of Rations from the 1st. Instant, be it more or less—

Col^o Malcom a few Days ago threw in his Resignation & went home-It was not accepted by Genl. Washington—

The Term of Inlistment for 9 of the Virginia Reg^{ts}. is expired & the greatest part of them gone home—

Genl. Varnum has begun to manoeuvre the Officers of the Division & means to continue it daily till they are perfect & then to manoeuvre the whole Division daily—
Fourteen Tons of Powder & 17 brass four Pounders have lately arrived at the Eastward.
As soon as Col^o Cortlandt's Reg^t. receives its pay I will stop part of Ben's money for you & send it together with your own Pay—I shall also Stop out of your Pay 23 Dollars 3/4 NYC which you can deduct out of Justices which I sent inclos'd to Stephen— I am Dear General with Respects to M^{rs}. McDougall & Stephen, Your most Obedient Servant

Margin note: If Stephen can be spared the latter End of next Month or beginning of March, I shall be fond of a Furlough for about 6 Weeks, if he'll relieve me, & if he cannot conveniently I will try to get one without—There is no Duty scarcely for me—Marvin acts as B Major to Genl. Varnum's Brigade—Col^o Pickering has left his Department & Col^o Scammel appointed in his Stead—

Source: Rosenbach Foundation, Philadelphia, Pennsylvania.

Clement Biddle to George Washington

Moorhall 25 Jany 1778.
On a Review of the Waggon horses belonging to the united States and those impressed or on hire in service with the Army, such numbers have been found unfit for Service that the Army will not only suffer for want of an immediate Supply of Provisions & forage but those horses belonging to the States now will be unfit for Service on the opening of the Campaign—A number of private Teams have been discharged, from their unfitness for Service, to replace which and to secure an immediate supply of Forage, I beg leave to propose to his Excellency the Commander in Chief that a request be made to the Legislative Council of this State to order at least one hundred & fifty waggons with four horses each to be furnishd by the different Counties agreable to the law passed for that purpose & that I may be informed of the places they can most conveniently rendezvous at, that I may give the necessary directions for them to be loaded with Forage & proceed to Camp here to continue in Foraging for such Term as the Council shall direct & until relieved by an equal number actualy arrived in Camp, that

no failure may happen in the necessary supplies of Forage—Without this Aid the Army must suffer greatly as the different Applications for waggons have failed & no Time should be lost in procuring the number requested—For the relief of the horses (the property of the States) now employ'd with the Army a large number will also be wanted which the Qu[r] M[r] Gen[l]. will point out.

The necessity of an immediate application to the Legislative Council is humbly submitted to his Excellency by His mo: obed sert

Source: John Reed Collection, Valley Forge National Historical Park.

John Laurens to Francois Louis de Fleury

Sir   Head Quarters 25th Jan[y]. 1778.

Both the Letters which you wrote, proposing different Plans for the destruction of the Enemys Shipping, were communicated to His Excellency—he applauds your Zeal for the Public Service and I have it in command from him to inform you, that he thinks employing some desperate fellows to use the sulphured Shirts [sic] would be the most likely way to succeed—he is afraid that the Scheme of the boats will be too easily frustrated; however as you seem to think so favorably of it, he gives you authority to make the experiment, getting such Advice and assistance from Commodore Hazelwood as may be necessary—the greatest Secrecy and Caution will be necessary, therefore the General does not require the formality of submitting your model to the inspection of any one, as the fewer the matter is communicated to the less likely it will be to fall into improper hands—prompt execution will likewise be advisable to give the less chance for discovery—if the Enemy have any notice of your design the guard-boats may without difficulty divert your fire-flats and render them harmless—

His Excellency desires me to farther a[ssu]re to you that rendering any importance Service in this way, will entitle you to the farther notice of Congress—I sincerely wish you Success and remain Sir Your most obed[t] Serv[t].

Source: George Washington Papers, Roll 47, Library of Congress.
Fleury was a Lieutenant Colonel of Engineers. He was then in New Jersey and had suggested ways to attack and burn the British ships at Philadelphia. Due to weather and other problems, none of his schemes were ever attempted.

Joseph Ward to Samuel Adams

Dear Sir   Camp January 26th, 1778

Your Favour by Mr. Dana I received from his hand as I met him, with Genl. Fulsom, the 24th Instant coming into Camp. Col. Pickering informs me he shall set out for York Town tomorrow or next day, I therefore embrace the opportunity to acknowledge the recipt of your Letter, and make some reply.

You may rest assured, my good Friend, that, if ever my political sentiments were right, they are so now; having never altered in any one particular that regards the civil Rights of the People.

And whereas in theory, I considered Standing Armies dangerous to Liberty, experience and observation confirm me in those sentiments; they are at some particular times a necessary evil, but an evil and a capital one, they always were and ever will be.

A good Militia, is my Doctrine, in the Camp and in the City; and so long as I own a pen, an hand, or an head, they shall be employed to establish a formidable Militia,—to render Standing Armies unnecessary, and to abolish them the moment they are not wanted.

They debase human kind, and lay waste the Natural and Moral World;—and therefore wise men will guard against them as much as possible.

As to "Schemes of Military Hierarchy", which "some have laid, and adopted", I conjecture that some of those you refer to have not come to my knowledge; for as I often combat such sentiments as tend to perpetuate an Amy, or to injure our Country, (in my humble apprehension) they are no perhaps so freely mentioned to me as otherwise they would be.

An Establishment of half pay for the Officers, I have often heard mentioned, and thus I hinted in a Letter some time since; some other lesser matters have also been hinted at a "Leisure" hour, for the encouragement of the Officers of the "Fighting Line", as the phrase is. The Establishment, so much talked of, is of such importance that I trust it will be well weighed before it takes place. If the war should be likely to continue so long, this measure may become necessary, by the absence of Virtue. But here this new Doctrine, is more generally received than any doctrine ever preached by St. Paul.

I rest satisfied that the Congress, will do respecting this matter what is best, when every circumstance is considered.

I have not had the opportunity yet to converse with Mr. Dana, upon the subjects you mentioned; but intend to wait on him for that purpose tomorrow. I have had very little acquaintance with this Gentleman, I saw him and had some conversation with him at Genl. Ward's quarters last year at Boston; he strikes, I believe, every one as a man of fine sense; and I never doubted but his Heart was as good as his Head. Genl. Ward gave me his Character in very bright Colours; and your authority confirms the sentiments I had before entertained. I believe he will render very important Services to his Country, in these days of trial.

Your propose for my consideration, "Which Army has been most busy about Rank &c" I have often made the comparison, with respect to this, & many other matters, (in my own mind) but as this does not remove the evil, it gives little satisfaction to one who feels for this army as well as that, and for his Country more than for either. I should oftener have written to you, and to some of your worthy Colleagues, during the Campaign, upon the dismal, if I have conceived it would have rendered any real service to the Cause we are engaged in; but I hate the tone of complaint, when it is not absolutely necessary, and knowing that Congress were surfeited with such stuff, I have been the more sparing on that head.

The Order for detaining Burgoyne's Army, which I believe will meet with general applause but whatever others may think of it, to me it appears to be the result of wise Council. What precedents, against it, the British plodders in musty records may be able to rake out of the ashes of oblivion, or from the filth of arbitrary Kingdoms, or from weak and trifling conduct of some feeble and irresolute proceedings of petty States in unenlightened times, I know not; but I am perfectly satisfied, that sound Wisdom, and strict Justice, and true Policy, will ever approve the Measure. Such Acts of national firmness spirit and independence, become us as a Free Nation; & we shall never be properly respected by others, until we thus respect ourselves. The violated faith & honour of British Generals, has long been a cause of suffering to many individuals, as well as injury to the public, therefore every good man must rejoice that Congress have now determined to compel those to be honest, by binding their interest, whom no ties of honour or motives of humanity could restrain from perfidy. I am happy in believing it will be a capital advantage to these States; it will compel the British Court, either to treat with us as a Nation, or to shew their villany to the world be refusing to ratify the capitulation of their General; if the first takes place we shall there by gain an important point, and if the latter, we shall secure so many prisoners for exchange, or any other purpose for which they may be wanted.

I had long revolved this measure in my mind, and wished it might take place unless there were some sufficient objections to it, but as it was so long delayed, I concluded that Congress saw farther than I could and thereby discovered some impropriety in the design. But I can easily conceive, advantage may accrue in consequence of it being delayed to the present time; the unexpected disappointment, may disconcert their future designs.

I have written several Letters to you since that by Mr. Gerry, but whether they reached you hands you did not inform me; they went by the Post. I shall do myself the pleasure to write by Mr. Dana, when he returns, if any thing in the mean time occur worth your notice.

I wish you the happiness of success in all your designs for the wellfare of your Country, And am, Sir, Most sincerely Your Obedient Humble Servant

Source: Samuel Adams Papers, Manuscripts And Archives Division, New York Public Library. Ward was Muster Master General with Washington's Army. His fondness for a militia over a standing army, was in opposition to the thoughts of most Continental Army officers.

William Bradford Jr. to Joshua Wallace

My dear friend,   Jan. 27th 1778. Valley Forge
I am happy in hearing from my brother that a communication with Ellerslie will be opened by means of the Expresses he will be obliged to send frequently to his principal M[r] Boudinot at Baskinridge. This will give me an opportunity of sending you the news of the Day, & of hearing often from you—The family at Ellerslie is so dear to me that my heart can ill brook suspence about their welfare—

You have probably heard of the late gallant behaviour of Cap[t]. Lee—The particulars are these—A party of Horse to the amount of 130 left Philad[a]. on the 20th Ins[t] & taking their rout thro' bye Roads suddenly surrounded the house where Lee & two Officers lay that Night—They were alarmed just Time enough to fasten the Doors—& post themselves & 5 privates at different Windows when the Enemy began a heavy fire thro' the doors & windows & demanded the immediate surrender of the house Lee, & his little party returned the fire with spirit—& tis said he had the Address to call out to them to surrender or that Morgans Infantry which was coming up would cut them in pieces—After a violent attack of 25 minutes, finding so gallant a resistance, & fearing lest their retreat should be cut off, they turned tail & made for Philad[a] They left several Caps & Pistols behind them which makes it probable the [sic] had several wounded—They took 5 of the troop prisoners who were out of the house & slightly wounded Lieu[t] Lindsay & Major Jemmason—Gen[l] Washington has thanked Cap[t] Lee & the Officers in the Warmest Manner—& An English Officer who lay in the house (being on parole & on his way to Philad[a]) speaks in Raptures of his bravery & proclaims it thro' the City. It is indeed remarkable that a Gen[l] & a Cap[t]. of the same name should be attacked in the same manner, & that the latter should repulse a party of horse 6 times as large as that which captivated the former—

What think you of the resolve of Congress for detaining Burgoyne—For my own part I look upon it as acting with a dignity becoming the free states of America—We have suffered our selves to be trampled on too long—Fie upon it. We declared ourselves free & independant & have hitherto suffered ourselves to termed [sic] & treated as Rebels—

What is your state doing towards filling up her skeleton Regiments If we do not exert ourselves with Vigor this winter, I fear we should not be able to dispossess the Enemy of Philad[a] And it appears clear to me, that if we duly exert our strength & bring the force into the field which we are able to do, we may crush them with ease & end the Content at once—Is it not extraordinary that with so many men as the Continent contains & with a proper sense of the importance of the object we are contending for, we should keep such a paltry army on foot, whose numbers have generally been inferior to, the handful that Britain send to subdue [worn]—When you take your seat in the Assembly & assist in navigating the political bark, I will write much more to you on this subject—

How does my dear Tacey & her darling Joshua? I am told she is unwell—and yet my heart laughed instead of being sad—Go on & prosper my noble brother!—My Landlord has read me so many Lectures upon the text of increase & multiply that I beg [to] think that he who begetteh a son covereth [a] multitude of Faults—He will scarcely allow all Paul's good Works, could attone for his continuing in a state of Batchelorism—

Give my warmest Love to Tacey—kiss the young Hero for me—& teach him to Love Your friend & brother

Source: "Selections From the Wallace Papers," *Pennsylvania Magazine of History and Biography* 40 (1916): 336-38.
Bradford was Deputy Muster Master General with Washington's Army.

Gustavus B. Wallace to Michael Wallace

D[r]. Sir   Camp Valley Forge Jany 27th. 1778
I have not for some time had an opportunity of writing you, indeed for this month past I have not been able. I was Just after Christmas taken w[h]. a fever that had like to have taken me of the stage the Doctors all give me out. but Jamey attended me night & day for six days. I turned the scales I am now confined to the house but gaining strength dayly willy stayed w[h]. me three weeks during my illness, and wrote you in the time he mentioned to you your sending me some cloaths by m[r]: Voroles the cloaths are two fine shirts & stocks two Coarse d[o] a fine d[o] printed Jeano waistcoat the one w[h]. the large [white] Spotts and if you can buy me two pair of coarse brown thread stockings send them I wrote you some time ago to buy me two pair of plated Spurrs which I hope you have they sell here for 10 dollars a pair I am now Maj[r]. 15th. V. Reg[t]. and bought a horse that I gave £ 60 for & since I have been sick my attendants have lost him. That has thrown me greatly back I think I am the most unlucky person in horses that ever was. I shall be obliged to buy another & they are very dear. you cant board now in a house in the Country under 10 dollars a week. The Enemy keep still in Philadelphia tho we scurmish w[h]. them now & then upon the lines I donot think I can come to Virg[a]. untill next fall when you may expect me if alive. pray do not neglect sending me those Cloaths or I shall be naked before May if m[r]. Voroles does not come out Cap[t]. Mercer will bring them over—put Windom in mind of the Meadow. My Complements to M[rs]. Wallace I am D[r] Brother you Most obd[t] Ser[t]

Source: Mss. 38-150, University of Virginia Library
Wallace was Major of the Fifteenth Virginia Regiment.

Thomas Bradford to Elias Boudinot

Dear Sir   Camp Valley Forge, Jany 28 1778
     Since your departure from Camp I have wrote you, by D^r
Wiggins of the 14th inst, & by Maj^r Forsyth of the 17th inst, since the
latter of which, my attendance on a Flag which came out from the City
with 11 Waggons of Cloathing &c for the Hessians & British Prisoners:
& my going down to the lines with two of Mr D. Frank's agents, has
taken up most of my time & prevented my writing you in the course of
the last week, as I intended.—This you will receive by Express, who has
with him a packet containing a number of Letters &c: which my late
initiation into Business prevents my answering & the propriety of their
being answered by yourself rather than your deputy, was he qualified,
induces me to forward them to you—N° 1 Letter of Returns of Prisoners
from Joshua Messereau dated Boston Jany 5—N° 2 Letter of returns
from Ezekiel Williams Weathersfield—N° 3 Letter from Thos Johnson
dated Annapolis Jany 11—N° 4 Letter from Joshua Messereau dated
Boston Jany 6—N° 5 Letters from Wm Atlee Lancaster Jany. 15 & 16
inclosing a letter & 136 Dollars for Maj And^w Galbraith New York—N^o
6 Letter from Robt Heaughy Jany 16 N° 7 Letter from Jesse
Hollingsworth—N° 8 Letter & Return of Prisoners from Daniel Hale
Albany Decr 7—N° 9 Letter from Ditto Decr 20—N° 10 Letter from
Congress—On N° 5 I have consulted Col. Harrison who says he will
mention to his Excellency the matter respecting returning the Invalids to
Genl Howe, when I shall write Col Atlee & at the same time shall
mention, that the Capt Wheatly mentiond by him is not to be found in
the list of the Prisoner sent out, therfore it is more than probable he is
numbered with the slain—By N° 6 Mr Haughy has rec'd the 1000
Dollars you left in my hands, & that he has been prevented sending a
part of your Order; this seems to have arose from a mistake; for his
Excellency has rec'd a letter from Genl. How informing him that he did
not mean to stop the flags by Water, but that previous Notice should be
given & passports obtained—this I shall write Mr Haughy—I have rec'd
the list of prisoners from M^r. Ferguson, which I have defered sending to
you till your orders, as I find it necessary for me. I have also rec'd a
Return of the Wants of the Prisoners which I shall endeavour to get
supplied as soon as possible—The Resolve of Congress in N° 10 I have
shown at the Commis^{ys} office therefore you can keep it or return it as
you please—

Cap[t]: W[m] Nichols of the *Eagle* came out with the flag on the 18th inst & was going for Reading being unable to affect the exchange for Cap[t] Manly but is since returned to Philad[a]: on a long Parole by order of his Excellency to try to be exchanged for Cap[t] Traverse of the *Raleigh* a 10 gun Brig belonging to Virginia—In consequence of the Golden Resolve, I have stopped & returned to M[r] Franks above £10,000 of paper money; his agents are in great want, he must therefore, in a short time send out his Gold—I shall take care to send the Cattle for the Prisoners on the first of Feby—I fear they want wood, but cannot learn for certain, as I have not had a line from M[r] Franklin—I should be obliged to you for an answer to the enclosed note from Gen[l] Poor, as it is out of my power to answer it, for Reasons before mentioned—On the morning of the 20th the Enemy sent out a large body of Horse (some say 130) who by a circuitous Rout got to Cap[t] Lee's Quarters & attacked the House just at break of Day but he with Maj[r] Jameson, L[t] Linsey (who is wounded in the hand) & 6 men beat them off with the loss of 3 of them killed & 3 or 4 wounded.—In their return they took 4 of Cap[t] Lee's men who were on Patrole—We are still as yet. The Enemy make small excursions 5 or 6 miles, but do no mischief—Col Broadhead with a party was at German Town a few Days ago & brot off a large quantity of Tann'd Leather—Your answer & further Orders will greatly oblige D[r] Sir Your Friend & Hum[ble] servant
P.S. Herewith you will receive several letters & six Dollars & ten English shillings for Cap[t] W[m] Scott of Col Clotz's Reg[t] of Lancaster County—

Source: Elias Boudinot Papers, Manuscript Division, Library of Congress.
Bradford was Deputy Commissary General of Prisoners, Boudinot's assistant.

John Fitzgerald to Walter Stewart

Dear Sir   Head Quarters, Jan[y]. 29th 78
His Excellency has received your favor of yesterday & thanks you for the information contained therein—By a letter from Major Jameson of 26th. Instant he mentions that Capt[n]. Howard has relieved Capt Craig at that Post & that he had wrote to Gen[l]. Pulawski for a Sett of fresh Men to do Duty there; this I expect will in a greater degree prevent the abuses which have been too frequently committ'd in the

Neighbourhood, by the too intimate Connexions between the Soldiers &
Citizens.

The General is fully of opinion that the Cloth belonging to such
persons as you mention should be taken for the use of the Army—
giving certificates of the quantity and quality to the persons to whom it
belongs, General Lacey has been directed to apply for the Quota of men
allott'd to that Post. I am & C^a

Source: George Washington Papers, Roll 47, Library of Congress.
Fitzgerald was an Aide-de-Camp to Washington. Stewart was Colonel of the
Thirteenth Pennsylvania Regiment. Stewart had written to Washington that he had
discussed with Lacey the problem of provisions going into Philadelphia in great
quantities. Stewart had suggested the seizure of cloth owned by Quakers, and stored in
mills around Newtown, Pa., in order to clothe his troops.

Jedediah Huntington to Joseph Trumbull

Dear Sir,   Camp Valley Forge 31 Jany. 1778
I am sorry to find you don't take your Seat at y^e. Board of
War—we did hope something from it—however wish you fairly out
of the Doctors Clutches, that you may give Your Country a Lift some
Way or other—your Name is mentioned with great Honour whenever
your quondam Department is on the Carpet which is very often—I
believe a new Comisary General will be appointed—
Nothing new has been stirring for several Days—a Com^{ee} of
Congress have been here since the 24th. Dana, Folsom. Herrvy of
Virginia G: Morris & J. Reed. a Gentleman or two from the Board of
War were to join them but I fancy they don't like us well enough to
come—
As it may be the Lords Time to work when we are at the
weakest, we have some Reason to hope for Deliverance, I am sure, we
seem to be doing, but very little for ourselves.
Conway, by hanging on & trumpeting his own Praise at York
Town, got a Major General and Inspector Generalship we did not like
the Man nor the Promotion, so we all agreed to put him in Country
and remonstrate to Congress, he very soon took himself off, and his
Constituents are, we hear, contriving what they shall do with him—
To the Institution of an Inspector General we had no Objection indeed
it was of our Recommendation—but the Man has rendered himself
very disagreeable—

The Marquis grows in our Love & Esteem as an Officer and a Gentleman.—

The Regiments which came here from Peeks Kill about the Time I did, have received no Ration money nor can they find any one who will look at their Accounts—

I did not think Parson Walter had Impudence enough to write you in that Stile—

The Affair of L¹ Col Dyer I have mentioned to Genˡ Varnum, he has received no letter from him on the Subject, what he will do with his Resignation I don't know—As the Place cannot be filled to Satisfaction at present for the Want of a proper Settlement of the Line of Field Officers for Promotion, I shall advise the Genˡ. to take the more Time—althou' it is a great Injury to the Service to have an Officer so much absent—

I have promised my self to get my Business done up by the last of February so as to visit my dear Friend in Connecticut—but I dare not be too sanguine in Expectations least some unexpected Event should stand in the Way—

4 February—

The Committee of Congress are still seting—have come to no Conclusions that are made known—believe however they will do something Clever Mʳ Morris—Dana & Herrvy are good Men and the other two for what I know may do well in this Business—

The British and Hessian Officers who came from the City the other Day with Clothing &C for their Prisoners at the Southward—passed Counterfeit Money & were guilty of some other Enormities on their Way the Board of War sent them back Bag & Baggage after having confined them a few Days—they are in high Dudgeon about the Matter—we hear Congress intend to stand up to the saucy Fellows with a little more Spirit than they have done—The Pensylvania Troops desert to the Enemy by the dozens but this entre nous—One Cause of Uneasiness among yᵐ. will soon be removed as they begin to receive Clothing. the Volunteers from Virginia we now hear are not to come—as they suppose it will prevent the filling their continental Battalions—they are taxing very heavily in that State—I think our Money will soon be on the gaining Hand—The Connecticut Troops will all want new Hats in the Spring—there is no part of their Dress affects their Appearance like this—I am much engaged that they should have a good Cock and that to preserve it they should if possible be bound with a strong Fillet of some kind or other—white or yellow will be the most eligible Colours—will you be kind enough to interest yourself a little in this Matter.

As this is the fourth page I will close with that—I am dear Sir Your and your Amelias most affect: Friend
I dont send Love to Nancy as I have wrote another Letter for that very Purpose

Source: Governor Joseph Trumbull Collection, Vol. 2, 167, Connecticut State Library.

George Weedon to William Palfrey

Dear Colo.   Valley Forge Jan: 31st 1778
I have a Regiment in my Brigade (the 6th Virginia) whose times of enlistment is now, (and will within the Course of ten days) expire)— The pay Master of it, tells me your Chest is already exausted and that he cannot get any money here to pay them of; This is a most unfortunate Circumstance and will be attended with bad Consequences unless you can give some Directions, or advice, respecting their pay. If it can be drawn at Lancaster or York, I will send the Paymaster with them to those places, I could wish them to leave the Service perfectly satisfied, as have hopes of their re-enlisting after a while provided they can be paid up to the time of their Dismission, and not kept in Service longer than they Contracted for. I am with due Respect Y^r. most obd^t Servt.

Source: John Reed Collection, Valley Forge National Historical Park.
Palfrey was Paymaster General.

Alexander Scammell to Timothy Pickering

Dear Col^o.   Saturday Night 12 oClock Feby 7 78
Col^o Gibson has informed me that you spoke to him about procuring me a Saddle—He says he can get me an elegant one made. If you have found a Saddler and bespoke a saddle & Bridle, (as you proposed in your Letter) at Yorktown I shall desire Col^o. Gibson not to buy me any at Lancaster. If not, otherwise—Please to inform me or him as you think most proper, or find suitable to your Conveniency—There is an Expedition I am inform'd going on at Northward, (which has

wasted away chief of our french Officers, Fleury amongst the rest) which I am apprehensive must prove abortive, unless Hea[ven] propitious whose ways are unfathomable should miraculously interpose in our Behalf. Two hundred miles through a desert to a place already exhausted of almost every necessary of Life Is a most difficult march for Troops at this Season the Year, more especially when its dependence must be upon traveling magazines. You are acquainted with the Reasons and Views much better than I am. Can you lay any plan to get Trumble or such another man appointed Commissary *Vice* the present one?— Can you find out some way to rouze the States to fill up the army seasonably? Cannot regular supplies of money and clothing for the army be furnish'd—Your good Judgement & perfect acquaintance with our situation is much depended upon—our prospects are gloomy at present; fatal Consequences must ever ensue unless the above Questions can be fully answered and complyed with. Y^r Affectionate anxious Friend

Source: Timothy Pickering Papers, Massachusetts Historical Society.
Scammell was the new Adjutant General, replacing Pickering who was appointed to the Board of War. The expedition referred to was a plan initiated by Congress to invade Canada. The Marquis de Lafayette, Baron de Kalb, Thomas Conway traveled to Albany, New York, to organize and lead the invasion, but there were not enough men or supplies to even begin the operation.

Joseph Ward to Richard Varick

Dear Sir   Head Quarters Feby 9th, 1778
        I wrote you the third Inst. in answer to yours of the 15th Ult. and requested, that, as a Body of Troops were soon to be in your Department on an expedition against Canada, you would continue to superintend the Northern Department, and that your Deputies would continue in Service with you. I now repeat the Request, lest by any means my former Letter should not come to hand.

        You intimated in your last , that you had thoughts of leaving the Department, if you should determine upon such a measure, you will please to give me the earliest notice of it that I may govern myself accordingly.

        But I sincerely wish you may find it agreeable to you to continue in the Department as I am well assured no New appointment would supply your place to advantage.

In theory, to one unacquainted with the Business, it may appear very easy to superintend & accomplish the mustering an Army, but Sir, you know it requires constant attention and vigilance to have it properly done.

However, I never expect any Gentleman to sacrifice in his better prospects to continue in any service, unless the circumstances are very peculiar. If, as I suspect, by continuing in the service, you must defer giving your hand to Miss <u>Schuyler</u>, I have not the insensibility to wish you to sacrifice so honorable and so sweet and enjoyment!—In every Scene, I wish you Felicity, And am Sir Yours &c

Source: Manuscript Department, New York Public Library.
Varick was Deputy Muster Master at Albany, New York.

Ephraim Blaine to John Ladd Howell

Sir   Camp Valley Forge 10th. Feby. 1778
You will imediately proceed to the Head of Elk and deliver M^r. Huggins his Letter requesting him without a Moments loss of time to forward all the Indian Meal and salt Provisions he has and Acquaint him how great our Demand is, the Meal is wanted imediatly for the use of the sick from thence proceed to Dover and Deliver M^r McGarment his letter and request him to use Every exertion to forward all the provisions he has by Water and Waggons, the Meal and salt Provisions being very much wanted beg you may assist him to forward the same with the greatest dispatch, when you have done this business you will return to the Head of Elk and there assist to forward the Stores till I come which will be near the Same time, I wish you a good Journey and am Sir Your Most Obd^t Servt

Source: Andre deCoppet Collection, Princeton University Library.
Blaine was Deputy Commissary General of Purchases, reponsible for purchasing food for Washington's Army.

Gustavus B. Wallace to Michael Wallace

D^r. Sir   Camp Valley Forge Feby. 13th. 1778.
I wrote you by G. Jones some days ago, all the news that was passing here then. but since that there has been a very remarkable

battle fought betwixt Lord Howe's fleet in Delaware & a fleet of Keggs sent down the river to blow up his lordships fleet by an old man from Rhode Island, this Battle was fought w^t. great bravery on both sides for a whole day when fortune seemed to declare itself in favour of His britannick Majesties fleet and army the formidable Fleet of Keggs being dispersed; (there seemed to be universal joy through the British army & fleet a foi de Joy being fired the day after & the City being Illuminated the night after then concluded their rejoicings in a Very Elegant Ball)—the fight being over Lord & S^r. W^m. Howe dispatched the swiftest in the fleet to Eng^d. to inform Ministry of this Signal Victory. this is a fact that may be depended on & you'l find it in the papers, where you'l find it explained—they say from London that the Mob has pulled down Lord North & Mansfields houses for Committing one of the Commons to the Tower. whom they released this is good news. there came out a flag the other day who it is said came to Know if the General wou'd make a general Exchange of prisoners. I can not tell what answer he got—

It is reported in Camp that Francis Lee made a Motion in Congress to Supercede his Excellency & was seconded by Sam Adams how true it is I know not but I suspected some thing of this kind ever since last winter these Motions will be attended w^t. bad Consequences for above two thirds of the Army wou'd be much dissatisfied, whose hearts are grafted in our great Commander—

I drew on you for 160 Dollars in fav^r. of M^r. Hungerford I was Obliged to do it. Having lost my horse shall be obliged to buy an other for I must neglect my duty which cannot be done w^t. out one & I suppose at a great price, I shall draw in April 1000 Dollars money the pay master owes me when I shall remit you what I owe you M^r. Hungerford wou'd not have asked for it but he wanted it to bring him to camp again [rest missing]

Source: Mss. 38-150, University of Virginia Library.
Wallace refers to the so-called "Battle of the Kegs," immortalized in the poem of that name by Francis Hopkinson.

Thomas Jones to Charles Stewart

Dear Sir   Camp Valley Forge Feby. 16th. 1778
     Am sorry to trouble you on so mellancholly a Subject as this. once more have we been driven almost to Destruction if not totally, the

troops in Camp have not Receiv^d. any Beef for 4 or 5 Days, Except Qua^r. allowance some days. a gen^l. & universal Complaint is Spread thro Camp and a Just one & no great sign of hav^g. it Relieved. its with the greatest Struggle that I have escaped bein Brought to disgrace oweing to the Neglect of M^r. Steenberger that let his men go 3 or 4 Days without flour or Bread, & plenty in Camp of that article at that time; I have had, & Blaine also, a Close Examination at head Quarters. four of those that Complain'^d, I had laid aside as they were Supplied with Bread & flour the Days they Complain'^d off [sic]. Col. Hamilton was appoint'^d by his Excellency to examin into this matter in order that the person who was in fault should be punish'^d he said in the Case of Steenberger I was to Blame for mentioning & giving him hard sooner then the men should starve, though he never mention^d of the troops Being really wanting, they have highly Condemn'^d Steenberger.—this you sa[y] let a person Slave toil & Drive about & do what he Can its all in Vain. he is liable to Suffer, as the fury of the Starved Soldiery may face him. tho' the Blame does not rest on me, as to my Part I shall not stay one hour longer than the 1st. next month, & desire you will Immediately Appoint another man in my Room, I Shall fall to Settle my Acc^ts. & see if I Cannot leave the Departm^t. with the same Credit as when I Came in, Col. Stewart I am serious in this matter & pray you will Not hesitate a moment in Coming to Camp, I dont Expect you will hardly find us all together when you Do Come. I Expect nothing else but every moment a Whole Brigade of the Starv'^d soldiers will Come to our Quarters & without Examining who is or what is not to Blame will lay Voilent hands on the whole of us: I am almost Desti[tute] there is 50 Barrells pork & about 40 D° herrings arriv^d. last night and M^r. John Phillips informs us there is 40 head of Cattle within 5 mile of Camp. This may Serve for to pay 2 days Beef &c. But they will have 3 or 4 days due them and when or where we will get the rest the Lord Knows. there is Expresses to be sent from Head Quarters this morning to all Quarters Capt. Lee with his troop is order [sic] to Elk from that to Dover to Impress all the teams Can be found & Bring Stores from that Quarter to Camp. we are ten times worst Situation now then ever you knewe us, not a waggon Can be got here to do any Business with they are all Engross'^d in the Q^r. M^r, & Forrage master Departm^t. there is only 2 small Brigades that Came from Lancaster [in] 3 weeks and upwards.—a Certain Gentleman (as Col. Blaine said) Contract'd Notions I am afraid has ruined the army. the Damn'^d Yankeys on this occasion gives the most trouble. shall give them a Hh^d. Melasses this day to each Division to see & keep one day more in tune, & some whisky or Rum to our Jersey and Pennsylvania veterans who I have not heard say a word all this time, I remain Sir—in the greatest Distress Y^r. most assured Friend & Hb^{le}. servt

Source: Charles Stewart Collection, New York State Historical Association.
Jones was Deputy Commissary General of Issues with Washington's Army. Stewart was Commissary General of Issues for the entire Continental Army. The food shortage in mid-February was the worst the Army endured during the six month Valley Forge Encampment.

Alexander Scammell to Timothy Pickering

Dear Col^o.   HQ Feby 19th 78
    A moments Opportunity presents of telling you our Distress in Camp has been infinite. In all the Scenes since I have been in the army, want of provisions these ten Days past, has been the most distressing, great part of our Troops 7 Days with only half a pound of Pork during the whole time—Our poor brave Soldiers living upon bread & water & naked exhibited a Sight exceedingly affecting to the Officers who were obliged to use their utmost Exertions to keep their men, whole Reg^{ts} nay brigades of the Soldiery sweering their pocks and in open Day declaring their Intention to go home. at the same time asserting that they could not do duty for want of food, which only induced them to imbody—A small supply has now arriv'd, but if ever provisions should fail in like manner, a Dissolution of the Army must take place inevitably. Desertions from the Enemy are very frequent—They lay still at present, and by what I can learn, they have from 11 to 29 men fit of Duty per Company in the marching Reg^{ts} & that they begin to be very sickly—Associations are form'd in these parts to apprehend all Officers they can kidnap, by some of the villanous Inhabitants of this State, several of them are apprehended & I hope will be hang'd—The most fatal Consequences will insue from the Deficiencies in the Commissarys & Clothiers Department unless immediately remedied by some means or other. should be happy to hear from you often. Y^r Very Humble Ser^t.

Source: Timothy Pickering Papers, Massachusetts Historical Society.

51

Hardy Murfree to Francis Lewis and John Pess

Gent^n. Valley Forge 20th. Feby 1778.
I rec^d. your Summons to com to York as an evidence against
Doc^r. Rickman. I should have com Imediately but was very unwell
and not able to ride that distance at this time, Captn. Wills is on
Command and has been this 7 or 8 days, I have sent Lieut^n Crittenton
Lieut^n. Gilaspie & Lieut^n. Cannon who was present when the Troops
was under Inocgulation. The N^o. Carolina Officers you sent for is all
gone to the State of North Carolina, I have Inclosed my Deposition
but I believe it will be on no Service because I was not at Alexandria
when the Troops was under Inocgulation, but com there som time
afterwards and heard the Officers & Soldiers Complain they had been
Neglected by Doc^r. Rickman, but I know nothing of it myself I was
Inocgulated by Doc^r. Rickman and Attended very well, I am Gent^n.
Your Hum^l. Ser^t.

Source: RG 360, Papers of the Continental Congress, M 247, Roll 101, i78, v19,
p129, National Archives. Murfree was Major of the Second North Carolina
Regiment. He had been asked to come to York to testify to a Committee of
Congress investigating complaints against William Rickman, who was in charge of
the hospital at Georgetown, Maryland. Rickman was exonerated of the charges
against him.

Hardy Murfree Deposition

Head Quarters Valley Forge Feby. 1778—
Personally appeared before me Hardy Murfree and Made oath of the
Holy evangelist of Almighty God—
That the 12th. day Novemb^r. 1777 he came to Alexandria in Virg^a. and
there found some North Carolina Troops under the Command of Col^o.
John Williams, the Deponent was Informed they had been
Inocgulated in the Month of Septemb^r. 1777—Som few days after this
Deponent was at Alexandria Col^o. Williams gave orders for the
Troops to March and said Doc^r. Rickman had reported to him that all
his men were able to March but one, Col^o. Williams asked this
Deponent if he would walk to the Barracks which he did, & on their
coming there found Three men very Sick and in a bad Condition,
Col^o. Williams sent for Doc^r. Rickman, the Doc^r. being not at home,
he sent an Officer for Doc^r. Parker, one of Doc^r. Rickmans Assistants

and asked the reason of all his men being reported fit to March but one, and them three so very bad—Doc^r. Parker sed them three men were never reported to him nor Doc^r. Rickman, Col^o. Williams then asked him if he never saw them men in the Condition they were in, he sed he had but as they was not reported Sick, he never gave them any thing, and the men being Almost naked Doc^r. Parker said it was not worth while to give them Physick when the men was so naked and lying on the cold Floor but said it was Nourishment they wanted. One of the Sick men had no clothing but one old Shirt and half an old Blankett—the other Two had some old Cloths—The Deponent further says that Night one of the men died and in some few days the other Two died and believes it was for want of Cloths to keep them warm and good care taken of them—

This Deponent was at the same time under Inoqulation and was attended very well by Doc^r. Rickman and his Assistants and further this Deponent saith not—

Sworn to before me Adam Boyd 2 nd. N. C. B.

Source: RG 360, Papers of the Continental Congress, M 247, Roll 101, i78, v19, p127, National Archives.

Walter Stewart to Thomas Wharton Jr.

Sir,   Camp, Feby 21st, 1778.

I am much concern'd to Inform your Excellency that an Express arrived in Camp yesterday afternoon, with the disagreeable news of a party of Light Horse belonging to the Enemy, consisting of about Forty, pushed up to Newtown, Bucks County, and took my Major, with a small party of men, Prisoners, and all the cloathing I have laid up there for my Regiment. My hopes of getting my Regiment genteelly and well cloathed this campaigne are vanish'd, unless your Excellency & the Council will assist me in it, which I must Intreat in the strongest manner. I really hop'd sir, my own activity would have saved you this trouble, but 'tis my misfortune to find all my good intentions frustrated by this most unlucky blow. My poor fellows are in a most deplorable situation at present, scarcely a shirt to one of their Backs, & equally distress'd for the other necessarys; but they bear it patiently, and however they may suffer for the want, I must say, I would rather wait a few weeks untill I could get all their cloathing together.

I now send Mr. Howell 22 lb Thread; 57 Groce Coat, & 42 Groce Vest Buttons; 326 5/8 yards Tow linin; 7 p'es Shalloon, & 4 p'es blue Broad cloth, Cont'g, 63 1/2 yards (trimmings I was sending to New town for the Cloths); these things I must request he will make the best use of in his power for my men; they are sufficient for the trimming of 300 suits cloathes, which I could wish to be blue and red if possible as I know White cannot now be obtained.

As I write Mr. Howel on the subject, I shall not trouble your Excellency farther, well knowing that every exertion is now making use of by the Council to have their Troops well cloathed.

I am with great respect and Esteem, your Excellencys most obed't hu'ble serv't,

New town is 24 miles from Philad'a, and the Militia are posted at Bustle Town, which makes this a most daring attempt on their side, and an unfortunate one on mine.

Source: *Pennsylvania Archives*, 1st. ser. (Harrisburg, 1854), 6:284.

Louis Lebique Duportail to George Washington.

Sir

M^r. de murnan, in whose favor I take the liberty of solliciting your kindness, has gone through the necessary studies for entering into the Corps of Engineers in France—he even obtained his licence for examination, which is never granted until satisfactory papers are delivered at the War Office setting forth that the person is of noble family. Frances does not receive into the Corps which is charged with the pretious Trust of her fortified Places and every thing that relates to the defence of her frontiers, any other subjects than those whose birth and education are pledges of their Sentiments and Conduct. This Licence is at the same time a proof of his Studies, because it can only be had in consequence of certificates given by professors who are liable to be called upon—The reason why this Gentleman was not admitted, was because the Arrangements of the Minister underwent a considerable change at that time—and that after having intended to make a considerable promotion in the Corps of Engineers, he confined himself to making a very small one—This Officer then entered into the Kings household Troops, but this Service not suiting his taste, which inclined him to engineering, he went to Russia which was then at war with the Turks. he there served in the capacity which he liked—he was Captain Engineer, but peace being made, he returned to France where he was preparing to reenter the Service when, called by some business to one of the Sea port Towns, The Enthusiasm which prevailed there in favor of this country took possession of him and he was persuaded to come here; a Vessel was ready, he embarked contenting himself with barely writing to his friends to recommend him to Me^{rs} Franklin and Dean, as well as to the principal Officers of his own Country here among others to the Mquis de la fayette, but none of these letters are arrived—

This Officer may be very useful here, he possesses sufficient theoretical knowledge to make him an exceedingly good Engineer, and he acquired some practice in Russia—he asks for the rank of Major, which appears reasonable. In all the States of Europe, a grade is readily given to an Officer and especially to an Engineer, whose Service is wanted, and it is easily conceived that this is necessary, as no one would expatriate himself and go into a new service with reaping a benefit from it—

I am with great Respect Your Excellency's Most humble And most obed^t Servt.

Source: George Washington Papers, Roll 47, Library of Congress.
Duportail, a Frenchman, was Brigadier General of Engineers. Murnan was given the rank of Major of Engineers in January 1779.

Jedediah Huntington to Andrew Huntington

Dear Sir,   Camp Valley Forge February 23^d. 1778
I will be glad to have you procure One hundred Bayonet Cases and Belts to buckle round the Waste on the cheapest Terms for money. least Hides can not be had—please to omit sending the Coats which I desired for Prentices Regiment—thank you for comforting Sister Nancy—I should in good Conscience come Home—but am very anxious to see the Accomplishment of many Matters of Consequence which are upon the Carpet, which I hope will not take up many Weeks more.

the Camp affords you no News at present, we have Reports of Diserters one Day that the foreign Troops are embarking, another Day that Howe is shiping off the new Levies to the West Indies, but we give not much Credit to what they say—however I think it likely they will show their green Coats some foul Play of other—not much Matter what goes with them.

give my Love to Sister and accept the same from your Aff^e Bro^r.

Source: Huntington Papers, The Connecticut Historical Society.

Samuel Carlton to Timothy Pickering

Dr Sir   Camp Valley Forge Feby 24th 1778
      I Receiv^d your kind favour of the 20th. Instant for which I Return you my Sincear thanks. when I had thos mortifying Minutes of parting with you (if my Memmory Serves me) I was Desir^d to acquaint you of any Grievances that we sustained now Sir permit mne to Acquaint your Honour, that we are in a most Deplorable Condition—Can you Believe me Sir, they are Eternal Truths, and much to be Lamented, that a Return of ye Regem^t was this Day Cal^d. for, and amongst Every man & mothers Son of them Could find no more Cloathing than what is hereafter mentioned—Viz, 10 Coats 12 Waistcoats 30 Shorts 10 p^r. of Britches 13 p^r. Stockings 16 p^r Shoes 11 Hatts & 80 Blankets—Good God is it possible—But why do I deny that, Do no my Eyes (to my Grieve) Behold it. Yes, Honourable Sir, and in the Bitterness of my Soul I must, and Say the Holy One of Israel (As I Can Imvoak no Greater Beig) I will proclaim [it] I will Discharge my Duty to God, my Country and the Soldiers—
      If we as officers have Common Merits Surely we should Blush to se those Verry Beings (on whome the Salvation of our Trysured Country Depends) So Barbarously Treated—
Permit me Sir to write you part of my Opinion (for I dare not write the whole) that if there is not soon Speedy Measures Gone into it will be attended with the most Fatal Consequences Our Soldiers have got Dissatisfied they find that are imposed upon, and have not Receiv^d. such things as was promised them at the time of their Inlistment, where the Failure is I Can not take upon me to Say, But this I Dare Assert—that there is a Gross Neglect in Some of the Departments—
Hond Sir, I am not a prophet or the Son of a prophet. But this I Dare do, to take upon my Self to prophesy for once That if there is not

Some Method Gone into, and that Very Speedily—Wo—Wo—Wo—
to America—
methinks by this time I hear you Say I and Tired of that old Fellows
Complaints, (But Still you will find them True, and I hope Before it is
Too late,) therefore shall putt the Ship about, and Stand upon the
other Tack.—I Receiv^d. a line from Capt Richd Ward of Jany. ye 15th
who inform^d me that your Good Lady & little Ta[d] was Well and
Desired to be Remember^d to you—
I have the pleasure to inform you that Genl Sulivan has So far
Accomplish^d. that Arduous Task of Erecting a Bridge over Skuil Kill
as far to pass over on foot—and have waited Some Days for planks
which by the Way is Verry Extreordinary [   ] Here is another Striking
Instance of Neglect, for had there Come propper Matterials the Bridge
would have Been finished long Since. which in my Oppinion is a
Mater Worthy you Gentlemon (Whom God in his infinite Mercy has
Appointed our Fathers) to Make some Enquirey about—I Could wish
to see Mr Whettmore, But if I should no have the pleasure of seeing
him please to Bear my Compliments to him—must Beg another
favour of your Honour, To Bear my Best Respects to the Honourable
Maj^r. Genl Gates and Could Wish (if not in this World in the World of
Spirits) to be under his Command again—I presume by this time you
May be Tired with my Nonsense—Honour^d Sir Must Beg leave to
Subscribe my Self your Obed [Servt]

Source: Timothy Pickering Papers, Massachusetts Historical Society.
Carlton was Lieutenant Colonel of the Twelfth Massachusetts Regiment.

Charles Scott to Allen McLane

My Dear Capt.　　　　　Camp at the Valley Forge 25th. Feby. 1778
　　　I rec^d. Your Favour by a Gent^n. who I did not know. I observe
Your Mentioning a person to whom I gave a pass. This Gentleman
was Strongly recommended to me as one of our Best Friends By
Col^{os}. Procter & North as He mentions to You—I can hardly suppose
That Ither of those Gentlemen would knowingly descive me, as for
the Gentleman I Know nothing of him my self nither Did I ever See
him, But sent him the pass By Col^o. Procter who told me he was
going The Next day in order to meet him at the White Marsh, and that
it was more than Probable, that it would not be conveniant to him to

come through the camp that was my Reason for granting the pass to a person that I never had seen—

However if You know him to be a bad Man or can git any good reason to believe So, You will (notwithstanding my pass) apprehend him.—I thank You for this Information, it will be a caution to me In Future. I am so hurrd that I hant time to Give You the little Nuse we have in Camp But Suspect M^r. Kelly will as I observe he is writing to You, I am pr[oud] to hear You are Successfull with reguard to Taking up Deserters,—Nothing is don With the Sixteen Reg^{ts}. Yet that has Transpired. I am My Dear Capt Y^r. Ob^t. Serv$^{t.}$

Source: Allen McLane Papers, The New-York Historical Society.
Scott was a Brigadier General from Virginia. McLane was a Captain in Patton's Additional Continental Regiment.

John Chaloner to Clement Biddle

Sir—   Febry 26 1778
The Brigades from Northampton County which you was kind enough to spare us to go to Elk arrived last evening,—where orderd to unload and go to your forrage Yard for orders—but instead thereof attempted to Cross the river and desert home, in which attempt several teams were lost and several men were drowned—the particulars of which we cannot ascertain as the teams that got over made their escape and is gone off—One of the Waggon Mr Michael Snyder is sent to you and hope he may meet with his deserts—He also accompanied the Teams across—but left his Horse in the river who returnd and is the occasion of coming back—I am Dr Sir your most hlbe Servant

Source: RG 27, Roll 13, Frame 895, Pennsylvania Historical and Museum Commission.

Robert Forsyth to Timothy Pickering

Dear Col°.   Camp Feb^{ry} 28th 1778
Your Man, Millet, is waiting; I have just Time to Tell you how exceedingly happy I was to hear of your being well.—I hope your situation is agreeable to your wishes and that your Last L^r. from

Home left your good Wife and darling Boy in perfect Health.—I stayed Twelve Days in Jersey found all my old acquaintance their in Peace and plenty—since I return'd have lived with General Greene his Aids are both gone Home. I have promised to remain with him, 'till Burnet come Back w^h. will be in a Day or two soon after he arrives I make a push for Virg^a.—I have got no appointment yet some of my Friends tell me I may rest satisfied that I will have one to my Wishes—

Lately Genl. Greene has been down towards Darby with 1200 Men— we swept off all the Horses, Cattle, Sheep & Hoggs the Waggons gears, Hay, Oats & grain some Leather and every Thing our Army wanted—I hope it will prevent the Enemy from making a Tour that way.—

While we were down 200 Men under L^t. Col^o. Ballard one Night endeavour'd to bring of the Hessian Picquett; but they got the Alarm and were in a large Brick House ready to receive them we had two or three Men slightly wounded. Major Days begs his Compliments to you farwell my dear Col^o. Your Affectionate,

Source: Timothy Pickering Papers, Massachusetts Historical Society.
Forsyth was Adjutant of the Fourth Virginia Regiment.

Elias Boudinot to George Washington

Dr Sir   Camp March 2 1778
        Having been detained in New York on the business committed to me by your Excellency, much longer than could have been expected, think it my Duty to take the earliest opportunity of Communicating a Report of my Proceedings and the Reasons of my Conduct—

        On my Arrival in Jersey I wrote to Sir Henry Clinton for permission to pass to New York, for the purpose of visiting our Prisoners &^{ca} as per paper N° 9 and received an Answer through Mr Loring which is in N° 10—When arrived at the City, was received with great Politeness and Civility, and put under no other restraint than being informed, that they trusted to my prudence for a proper behaviour—

        My business here being to inquire and find out the real State of our unfortunate Brethren, and not to negotiate any general

Principles I thought it prudent in the first Place, to make it a point to know the Tempers and Characters of the particular Persons I have to do with, and then endeavour to improve it to the advantage of our miserable Prisoners—

Having for several Days visited the different Places of their confinement, and made every Inquiry in my Power; I beg leave to report to your Excellency the result of the whole—That I found the Hospitals in tollerable good Order, neat and clean and the Sick much better taken care of than I expected—That the Sugar House appeared comfortable and Warm, having a Stove in each Story and Shutters to the Windows—The Prisoners also being well Cloathed and each of them having a good Blanket, may stand through the Winter very well, especially as they are not crouded, being now reduced in the whole to about 400, two hundred of whom, are in the Sugar House; the rest being in the different Hospitals—Some of the Privates appear to be a sett of sad Villains, who rob each other of their Cloaths and Blanketts, and many of them sell their own Shoes, Blanketts, and even Shirts for Rum—

That the Provisions for the Privates are Issued in the proportion ma[rked] in Paper N° 5—

That in the Provoost, I was greatly distressed, with the wretched Situation of so many of the human Species—That on meeting all the Prisoners of War together in a Room, in Company with Mr Loring I heard their Complaints and took Notes of the Accusations on which they were severally confined in order to found a Representation to Major Genl Robertson in their favour—They repeated to me instances of the most shocking barbarity in presence of the keeper of the Provoost, whom they charged as the Author—As the beating and knocking down Officers of Rank and distinction on the most triffling Occasions, locking then up in Dark, damp Dungeons, for asking more Water than usual in Warm Weather; or for not going to bed immediately on being ordered by the Serjeant—Officers have been locked up in the Dungeon for examination, and left there without farther inquiry, or any Charge brought against them for many Months—That besides Prisoners of War, there are many inhabitants here, as Committee Men, Commissioners, Oppressors of the Friends of Government &^{ca} &^{ca} who are wretched beyond description—That Inhabitants and Persons in Civil Departments when taken, are sent to the Provoost without distinction, and at present there seems to be no redemption for them—

That on my stating the Case of each of these unhappy men as contained in Paper N° 2 and delivering it to General Robertson, he very humanely agreed to the discharge of all the Officers (excepting seven) on their Parole; and gave me the strongest assurances that he would not allow of such a Power in the Serjeant of the Provoost, but would put a stop to it immediately—That the Officers on Long Island, are boarded out amongst the inhabitants, in the most convenient Manner, and appear to be very comfortable and Healthy They amount to about 250—

They have been completely cloathed and money advanced to them for other Necessaries, to the amount of about £30 per Man.

That there have been issued to the Offices and Privates Cloathing as per Return N° 11—

That on a rough Calculation; I am now in advance, and indebted upwards of £22,000 for the Cloathing Board &^{ca} which is daily accumulating at the Rate of 500 Dollars a Week for Board only—

That to answer the pressing Necessities of our Prisoners I have been obliged to stretch my Credit to the Utmost—That not being able to obtain the least Aid from the State of Jersey, have been put to the greatest difficulty to make remittances, not being able to procure above 300 Barrells of Flour, for want of means of Transportation; and altho' I have employed the best men I could meet with for the purpose, can get nothing done effectually without my personal attendance—

That finding the officers running into unnecessary Expence for mere Ornament and finery, by which Debt would greatly accumulate, and the difficulty of making remittances increased, I put a Stop to it by orders as p^r N° 6—

That from the Enemies returns of Prisoners (which I rather think to be large) there are 50 Officers at Home on Parole—235 on Long Island—8 in New York—46 deserted their Paroles—282 Privates at Home on Parole—1821 Privates in dispute and 451 in the Sugar House and Hospitals—

That on attending the Provision Store and examining the Provision then issuing, found the meat tolerably good, the Biscuit musty and indifferent, but the same as issued to the British Soldiers—

That the Provisions are divided by persons chosen by the Prisoners from among themselves, and if not embezzelled in the Carriage from the Store, must be received by them in the Proportion allowed—This might be prevented by a Subaltern Officer on his Parole, attending the issuing and Carting—That I have allowed the Privates an addition of two Pounds of Beef, and as much Bread per week, making up in the whole, a full Ration p^r man p^r Day—Also as much Wood as is necessary for their Comfort, which has saved the Lives of many, this Winter, who otherwise must have perished—That altho' the above appears now to be the State of the Prisoners in New York, from my personal Observation, which visiting the several Departments; yet I think it my Duty nevertheless to add to this Report, which I received from the unanimous representation of both Officers and Privates— Viz^t That this Alteration has taken place within a short time past, in a great Measure by the Industry and attention of Mr Pintard our Agent in New York, who has employed special Nurses in the Hospitals, added to the supplies for the Sick, and done every thing in his Power for the relief of the unhappy sufferers (Vid Dr Mallets Letters on the Subject of Nurses N° 8) But Mr Pintard being forbid going to the Provoost, his Care cannot extend to those confined there, except as to sending them Provisions, and fire Wood—

That on applying to General Robertson, for carrying into Execution the Agreement relative to the Exchange of Prisoners on Parole, as far as the Officers sent into New York would apply; and particularly for liberating Major Genl Lee, in Exchange for Major General Prescott who had arrived in New York several Weeks past; received for Answer, that General Robertson know of no such Agreement having never received any Information or instruction from Sir William Howe on that subject—

That having repeated my Applications for the relief of the seven remaining Officers in the Provoost, I could not succeed, and as the objections ag^t the liberation of Smock Whitlocke and Skinner are rather triffling and they being exactly in the same predicament, with the Officers lately taken on Staten Island, it is but Justice due to these unhappy Men, immediately to confine those officers Prisoners with us, on the same Principles—That the Officers on Long Island conceive it would be greatly to the public Advantage to perfect a general Exchange, even at a considerable loss, as the great Number of our brave countrymen who daily fall a sacrifice to the severity of their Captivity, call loudly for speedy relief. The Principal Officers also assure me, that the Privates in dispute were sent out by General Howe, in consequence of their earnest Application—

That having had several Conversations with General Robertson on the Subject of the Prisoners, he urged the Settlement of the past Board,

due from our Officers, as it has not been paid by Genl Howe—He
admits the Propriety of the mutual Accounts being speedily liquidated
and the Ballance paid, as by that means the inhabitants will be
induced to treat them with greater kindness—That on Letters arriving
from Genl Howe, relative to the Orders issued by us, for preventing
their purchasing Provisions with us West of New Jersey, General
Robertson thought that Genl Howe must have misunderstood the
Matter; and therefore desired me to state the Facts, which I did a
Copy whereof is in Paper N° 4—General Robertson approved of a fair
Barter of Cloathing for Provisions so that it was not abused to the
fitting out our Men for a Campaign and proposed (to obviate the
difficulty) the leaving the Blankets of every exchanged Soldier, with
our Agent for the use of the Prisoners remaining behind—That with
these letters from Genl Howes orders also came for sending Genl Lee
by the first Man of War to Philadelphia to give his Parole to Genl
Howe in Person—I objected to the impropriety of a Winter Passage,
when a Journey by Land was so much shorter and easier, but as this
could not be done without farther Orders, General Robertson wrote to
Genl Howe on the occasion and General Lee being anxious and
uneasy, begs your Excellencys interference as speedily as possible—
That after finishing the Business of the of the Military Prisoners, I
waited on Commodore Hotham, and informed him that Mr Pintard
having obtained Provisions and Cloathing for Sea Prisoners had been
refused the liberty of sending them on board of the Prison Ship[s]
notwithstanding the pressing Necessities of those suffering People.—
He informed me that he could not know Mr Pintard, or any other
Person but his own Commissary, and that he would not suffer any
Cloaths purchased in New-York to go on board without Lord Howes
express Orders, but that any Provisions sent to the Commissary
appointed by him, should be distributed I applied then for the
enlargement of the Sea Officers on Parole, but he answered that this
could not be done, as no Sea Prisoners were ever admitted to that
Indulgence—
Having obtained permission, I visited Captain Manley on board the
Preston, who appeared dejected with his long and close
Confinement—That on earnestly soliciting his Exchange for Captain
Furneaux of the Syren, was informed that it could not be done without
orders from Lord Howe—
That there are 58 Officers and 62 Sea Men on board the Prison Ships,
who suffer greatly and die daily vid N° 7—That on my Arrival at New

York I was distressed to find, that the most unfair and ungenerous partial Exchanges had been and was then carrying on from the State of Connecticut, Mr Joseph Webb was then there the second time by Virtue of a Flag of Truce from Govr. Trumbull whereof is N° 1 That on finding a Number of Officers and privates exchanged by Mr Webb, contrary to their due order, I put a stop to it and directed the oldest in Captivity to take their place. That the difficulties arising from this Practise, not only as to the Confusion it causes in my department, but also in the Jealousies and uneasiness raised among the other Officers, call for immediate relief—

That it has been proposed for the purpose of healing all past breaches, and putting the affairs of Prisoners on a proper footing, by a general Exchange, that Persons appointed by your Excellency and General Howe shall meet together near Philadelphia and make a final Settlement of all disputes relative to Prisoners and negotiate a Cartel in future—

I cannot close this Report, without taking Notice of the Candour and Politeness with which I have been treated by Genl Robertson, Mr Loring and the Gentlemen with whom I had public Business in New York

Permit me also to assure your Excellency, that notwithstanding I have unexpectedly taken up so much time in this Business yet that I have not wasted a Moment that could be avoided: the many delays necessarily attendant on services of this kind especially with Gentlemen who have so many other Avocations, would have given me more uneasiness, had I not know that no other Employment could have given you more satisfaction than relieving the distresses of our miserable Captives—How far I have succeeded, the list of Prisoners entirely relieved (N° 3) and the Prisoners themselves will best determine—

In order farther to satisfy you on this Head, as well as to possess you with every Transaction on this occasion—I enclose a Journal of them kept to assist my own Memory while in the City—

If I have been so happy as to merit your Excellencys approbation, shall think my Attention, Labour and fatigue amply repaid—

I have the honor to be with great respect & Esteem. Your Excellencys Most obed humble ser
PS I had almost forgot to mention that having received the fullest assurances from our Officers, that a poor Woman had saved the Lives

of a Number of our Prisoners by exerting herself in serving them far beyond her Abilities, and that she was now in a suffering Condition for want of Provision, I thought it prudent to send her a Present of 5 Barrels of Flour—

Source: Princeton University Library.
Boudinot's letter gives a good idea of the problems inherent in his position, and the hardships suffered by American prisoners. At this time, each side was expected to feed and clothe its men held by the other side. Officers who had given their paroles, or promise not to escape, were usually allowed to board with families in the locale where they were being held.

Israel Shreve to Mary Shreve

Dear Polley—   Camp Valey forge March 3rd 1778.
A Week ago this Day I Returned to Camp from Jersey, and Received a Letter Dated Six weeks ago, and sent by Colo: Becker, this Letter was Rather Sevear, and full of Complaints, But upon Recolection Remember I sent one to you Dated the 20th of January By Capt. Becker, about the same time you Wrote that to me, and hope that Releaved you for the present But by this time you must be in Want again, which Gives me Great uneasyness, was in hopes I Could Git Leave to Come home for a few Days, but General Maxwell has got Leave to Go home for three weeks & is to Set off tomorrow, when the Command of the Brigade falls to me untill his Return, when I Will Come home If possable, a few Days. I Send this by Mr Osmun my Quarter master, with three hundred Dollars A Sum I hope will Last you a Little while, I hope to Supply you Better in future I am Likely to have forty Dollars a month aded to my present pay. I hope by this time Chuff and the Children is in Better health, and yourself, Please to Send me two more Shirts and one Stock and the Coat I Left At the Taylors, the Letter I Wrote by Capt. Becker mentioned your coming to Camp If you Could Convenient, I shall Quarter while maxwell is Gone at Mr John Mitchels where Maxwell now Quarters A Genteel Place (the Day before yesterday I had the honour to Dine with General Washington and his Lady. Yesterday I Dined with Lord Sterling and his Lady.) Do I Desire pay all your Dets in Reading As soon as you Receive this, Write me a Letter by Osmun and tell me just how you Are in every Way, and whether you Can Conveniently Come and See me or not for one or two Weeks, I shall have a Good

House &c. As Colo: Brearly and I Came from Jersey we were near being taken by the British light horse, But happaly escaped,

Give my Compliments to Mrs Sullivan, Miss Peggy, Miss Kitty, & all my friends at Reading. I am your faithfull and Loving Husband

P.S. when I was in Jersey I was at Coopers ferry heard from Mrs. Williams, who was well, I was at Woodberry Polley Wood and Mary Branson Desired to be Remembered to you, Woodberry Looks very Distressed, my Relations in General was well and mostly Desired to me Remembered to you, If Capt Balding is alive Do Let me know how he is,—I come across Some pins and send you a pound they Cost fifty Shillings and Some thread that Come in my way

Do Let me know when your Last orders is out for provisions and for Wood.

Source: *Pennsylvania Magazine of History and Biography*, 39, no. 3 (1915): 376-77.

James Bradford to Thomas Wooster

Dear Sir   Camp the 4th. 1778

Agreable to your request I have waited upon Co^l. Palfrey PayMaster General and his information was that as General Wooster was in the Northern Department and he could not ascertain the time of his last PayMent he would not pay it and for which reason he made the remark at the bottom of the Account of which a Copy you may find at the Foot—and refered me to his Excellency the Generals information was that; he agreed with Co^l. Palfrey: and that you must gett a Certificate from the PayMaster General of the Nothern Department (which I am informed is one M^r. Trumbell) wether General Wooster ever received any Pay in that Department (and if any) the Date of the last Payment—and to prevent giving you any more trouble after this: his Excellencys Secretary Co^l. Harrison thinks you had better procure from the Paymaster of the Middle Department (if any there where [*sic*] at that time) a Certificate for the same purpose as mentioned Above; provided you may think the Certificate you gett from M^r. Trumble not a sufficiency—the Account still remains at Head Quarters unditumined wether your Father is to receive any Pay as Major General: tho your instructions upon that head shall be obeyed, and a Certificate from Co^l. Palfrey (provided he is not allowed the Pay of a Major General) shall be obtaind: and forwarded to you—I should have wrote you before but could not gett the business settled sooner: and therefore have taken Care to forward a Copy of this to you at Fish Kill. this is to be forwarded you by Co^l. Chandler: who will take some pains that you may receive if safe.—As the Army its thought will not take the Field before the Middle of May, think you have best not loose any time about your procuring the necessary Certificates for the settlement of your Fathers Account: and as the Army remains quiet and will until the first May think you had better imbrace the present opportunity: upon the Certificates being produced from M^r. Trumbell at Head Quarters, His Excellency inform me that the Account should be immediately paid and no further trouble given you.—I hope long ere this reaches; you and your Amiable Lady with Miss Brashes, & Miss Sheldon are arrived safety in Newhaven: where I sincerely wish you all the happiness a Marriage State can possess: I need not relate to you the disagreable journey I had in getting to Camp—as it was Truly disagreable attended with a serious of [sic] bad Wether: and should much rather have prefered your agreable company of a Bottle of M——Your kind offers to me: I shall ever esteem: and shall ever be remindfull to retaliate them: tho should I leave my present department: and accept of an offer upon an uncertainty sure you will readily agree that I should prefer the former in preference to the latter—tho' as the Army are to be in for course of a few days New Moddled am not yet determined upon staying—and hope, should any think [sic] turn up that may be to my advantage, trust your worthy friendship to inform me—As to New we have none here, the Armys both remain peaceable; only their partys of Horse now and then make excurtions into the Country: and was so kind as to take the other day 133 Head of Fatt Cattle which where [sic] from your part of the Country and distind for the use of our Army.—they had been down in NJ as far as Salem and Totally destroyed it.— Nothing now remains further for your attention: hoping that my proceeding may meet your approbation—and with sincere wishes for you and your worth [sic] Ladys happiness believe me to be—Yours to Serve

P.S. There will be an error in the Account of 24s. which I will explain to you upon the settlement of the Account—Pray Present my best respects to the Two Ladies in your family: and let them know that I hope their wishes are fully answered by going to Newhaven—That

Miss S——had the pleasure of Co[l]. W——most agreable Company: and Miss B——has met with some Genteel and Worthy Acquaintance that will make their stay will you much more agreable than they could realy immagin—I am sure Miss S——will think so when she has the Addresses of Co[l].——Excuse my Bad Writing As I am I a hurry: do not neglect writing me—I shall send you P[er] Post to Fish Kill and Newhaven Copy of this.—

General Wooster having served in Another Department I cannot judge wether this account is right or not the propriety of it's being paid must be determind by His Excellency General Washington—

Was Signed W[m]. Palfrey PMG.

Dear Sir   10 March 1778
        Since writing the Above have but little to add, only that as there is no Money expected as this Place very soon, think you had best be as expeditious as possible in the settlement of your accounts, as the Ready Rino is not at all times to be had here—I hope you will write me how to proceed and if my proceeding meet your approbation, which I shall be happy to hear of—let me hear of the welfare of your worthy Lady who I long to see; and happly blest in her situation: as not doubt she must now be so—I am
Excuse haist and bad writing—

Source: John Reed Collection, Valley Forge National Historical Park.
Bradford was Quartermaster of Patton's Regiment. Thomas. Wooster was a Captain in Samuel Blatchey Webb's Regiment. His father, Brigadier General David Wooster, had been mortally wounded in April 1777.

John Else to Samuel Gray

Sir   Camp March 4th. 1778
am Extreamly Sorry it was not in my Power to Send a Return Sooner. but Could not, on account of M[r]. Douglass having the books in his Care and on his way to Camp had the misfortune to Loose them and Some Papers of Consequence, however the Returns I believe Came safe to hand, he having Put then into his Saddle bags, the Others he says was Ty'd in his Great Coat behind him, I have Ent[d]. the Returns

and I believe Sent You an Exact Return of Stores Issued—but the Stores Rec^d I am not able to Send at Present but hope it a Short Time to have to Pleasure to Se You at Fishkill when I Shall Endeavour to Put my affairs in as good a Posture as Possible I have Quit the Division and am at Present at the Com^y. Gen^{ls} Quarters Settling my affairs

I Dont know of any thing I Shall be at a Loss for but the account of stores on hand the first of September which You Once saw Drawn Out the Other Stores I have from M^r. Fitch & Worthington Only—I am Sir with Respect Your hb^l. Servt

Source: Samuel Gray Papers, Connecticut Historical Society.
Else was an Assistant Commissary of Issues with the Army. Gray was the Deputy Commissary General of Issues at Fishkill, New York.

Enoch Poor to Meshech Weare

Sir,   Pensylvania Valley Forge Camp 4 March 1778
The goods you sent by Mr. Nichols Came safe to hand, which was very acceptable, though inadequate to our wants. (as you may see by the enclosed return) But it seems by the accounts you receive from those that arrive home the roads have been crowded with teams carrying clothing to the army so that by this time you may conclude we are fully supplied, but Sir, I would inform you these waggons arrived a few days ago and there has since been a division made of all the clothing in the Continental Store, according to the present wants, and we received one coat to the 100 of our wants, waistcoats 6 to the 100, Breeches 4 to the 100, shirts 2/9, shoes 1/3, stockings 1/5, blankets 2 to the 100, so that our army still remains in their ragged suffering situation, and I fear we shant be better supplied until the several States will take the matter into their own hands and appoint an agent for each State, to collect the clothing proportioned to each Town, and forward it to the Army, but so long as we depend upon the Continental Commissaries for Clothing I fear Our Complaints will encrease the want of clothing and the Scarcity of provision this winter has made our situation very disagreeable, and what adds to our distress, the small pox got so into our Camp were obliged to innoculate our men, I have near five hundred from your State now under the operation and not more than One half of them have a blanket or any kind of covering except Straw, how they will live through this cold season God only Knows. The shoes sent by Colonel

Hunt came safe to hand. The resolve you have passed respecting supplying the soldier's families gives great relief to the minds of many amongst us—I shall use my influence with the men to send what money they can spare, I have nothing new to write—I beg you would hurry on the Officers & Soldiers to Camp—I am sir with great esteem your most obedient humble Sert

N.B. Those officers who came home from Canada this winter are exchanged.

Source: Peter Force Mss, Ser. 7E, New Hampshire Miscellaneous, Library of Congress. Weare was President of the State of New Hampshire.

Jedediah Huntington to Jeremiah Wadsworth

My dear Col.   Valley Forge March 5, 1778
    Your acceptable Favours of the 25th. of last Month, 9th and 19th of this are in my hands, the two former would have been acknowledged before this Time had I not heard you was expected this Way—I am under the Exercise of great self Denial in keeping myself from my Friends, <u>One</u> in particular, but the Condition of our Affairs here seem to demand it—in a few weeks however I hope to see an Alteration in them favourable to my private as well as public Wishes—The Situation of the Com[y]. Gen[l]. Dep[t]. is shocking—do put your Hand to it, will you? shall I not have the Pleasure of Seeing you here soon on your way to Congress to tell them what ought to be done.

    I have asked several Times who is to succeed G——Spencer but cannot learn—I have as little Hope as you from the Regulations of Prices, indeed I have no Hope at all—since I wrote you about Paper my Q[r] M tells me he can get any Quantity hereabouts I thought that Article was scarce here because we were not duly supplied & got the Gen[ls] Leave to supply my Troops as I could—but it seems that the fault lay with the Q M[r] Gen[l]. or one who stiles himself such. this Dep[s]. as evil as the other is wretched—

    There is no Party, as you have heard, in the Army. the General and subordinate Officers were never better agreed in this or I believe in any Army in the World—there is a rascally Party out of the Army aiming to injure some of the best Characters in the Country.—but their little paltry Pollicy and Cunning begins to be despised and will defeat its own wicked Purposes—

I heartily rejoice that our worthy Friend is better his Presence is very necessary to the Board of War—

I told Fanning to tell you the Reason of my not writing You—I have never rec^d the Spirit—its no matter—dont promise my self any thing but Disappointment from the northern Expidition—I shall be sorry to have the Marquis's Character Suffer as he is very clever—

If I can get Time you shall have more Scribbling from your Sincere & aff^e Friend

Source: Jeremiah Wadsworth Papers, Correspondence, Connecticut Historical Society. Tilghman was describing the "Conway Cabal." an alleged plot involving Generals Thomas Mifflin, Horatio Gates, and Thomas Conway, as well as some members of Congress, to remove Washington from command of the army. There is no hard evidence that such a plot existed.

Ezekiel Sanford to George Washington

May it please your Excellency   Camp 7th: March 1778

Actuated by the purest Sentiments of Friendship to my Country, and with a Determination to sacrifice every thing In the sacred cause of Freedom I was induced to accept of a Commission in the American Service, which I have (I flatter myself) sustain'd with some degree of Honor, but finding myself at many times by reason of bodily infermities unfit to perform my duty—which together with the peculiar Circumstances of my Family and Domestic Affairs—And as the present plan or New Model of the Army will make many Supernumerary Officers—For which reason I am induced to ask Your Excellency, for a Discharge from the Service.

But as the giving in of Commissions is in my Opinion a reflection upon an Officer, as tho' he was unworthy to sustain it, I would beg your Excellency's Indulgence, in holding mine in my own hands—This particular favor will be ever gratefully remembered—My Your Excellency ere Long crown'd with the Laurels of Victory—Return to enjoy All the sublime pleasures of Domestic Life, in the full possession of Peace and Freedom

Is the Wish of him who is with the most perfect Esteem—Your Excellency's Most Obedient & Obliged Hum: Servant

I have no Objection to make to Capt Sanfords being discharged—
                    J. Huntington B Genl

Source: RG 93, M 859, Roll 2, # 696, National Archives.
Sanford was a Captain in the Fifth Connecticut Regiment. His resignation was effective on March 17.

James Mitchell Varnum to Nathan Miller

Sir—   Camp Valley Forge 7th March, 1778
        This is Saturday Evening; My thoughts have been religiously employed the whole day; Reflection is very agreeable upon such Occasions; but the Result may become so serious as to produce a Fixed Melancholy unless the Mind can be sufficiently unbended. To disclose our Feelings to our daily Familiars, does not afford the Relaxation necessary; We must [therefore] call to View an old Friend: This will give a temporary Relief; For the whole Space of Time requisite for the Intelligence to reach him will be spent in dubious Agitations; without a fixed Sentiment of what Judgment he will form: Previous to a Knowledge of his Opinion the Sadness is removed, & we begin anew upon the Score of thinking. Under this kind of Operation I have ventured to address myself to you, well knowing that in every serious matter you will feel a past as becomes a Brother and a Friend.
        My religious Exercises, you must know, are the Result of Fear; I am certain you was never religious upon any other Principle; certainly Therefore you can sympathize with me. My fear is that of dying in a heathenish Land, deprived of a Christian Burial. Should that befall me, how can my Body be found by those who are convenant only in holy plac[es] and with good Beings?—You are well acquainted that a Man must die when his Time comes; & should mine approach while confined in Pennsylvania, how can my Soul find its Way thro this Tory Labyrinth, to a pure Ether, congenial to its own Nature?—As you are well versed in mystical Theology, I must beg an Answer to these important Queries. If you comply, Generocity will mark your Conduct, and a regard to sage Experience Will give Weight to your Decision; But should you refuse, an Argument will stand against you of an infallible Apostasy.
        Was I to be confounded in my Reveries upon the Season; Was the Law of Motion in the Heavenly Orbs to depart from my intellectual Powers, to whom could I apply but an Imlack to put be right; In the present Difficulty, where shall I direct my Attention but to <u>Nathan</u>, a

Prophet of late, who has trod the crooked Paths & [precis]ely surveyed their various Windings.—

Another Question, of less Consequence however, I must propose, whether the Devil contouling the Inhabitants of one State, few excepted, can be at Leisure to preside in, or capitally influence others at the same Time?—This is a matter of some Consequence, as I think you, in Rhode Island, are in a State of perfect Freedom; but if he is perfectly diffusive, and looses nothing by influencing much, then you may feel some of his crafty Wiles. Be it as it may, will not his very extensive Employment soon make him sick of his Commission, & induce him to resign his Office?—That is momentous, as it concerns you and me much.

I hope these scattered Thoughts will not essentially divert you from your more valuable Employments, but, in some Measure add to your innocent Amusement. With Esteem [for] the Worthy, I am your Friend & Servant

Source: Houghton Library, Harvard University.
Miller was a Colonel of the Rhode Island Militia.

Israel Angell to James Mitchell Varnum

Sir   Camp Valley Forge March 8th. 1778
        Whereas Lt Joseph Whitmarsh of Col^o Greenes Reg^t has apply'd to me for a Recommendation for a discharge from the Servis, for the following Reasons, 1st as the Settlement of the Rank in the Reg^t. now Stands, Seems Agreable to the Field Officers, and he would by no means wish to create any uneasiness in the Reg^t. as it would Destroy the end and designe of his Entering the Servis. 2^{ndly} under his present Sittuation he cannot be easy, and the Removal of the cause would be very Disagreable to many of the officers in the Reg^t. by which means it would make his Case unhappy, for these Reasons he Choses to retier from the Service, (Although Lt Whitmarsh is a good officer) Considering the above Circumstance Shall Recommend him to your Honour for a discharge, and give it as my opinion that he ought to have an Honorable one,
        I am Sir your most obd^t Humble Servt.

Camp March 8th 1778.

L. Whitmarsh is hereby recommended for a Discharge from the Service.

J M Varnum

Source: RG 93, M 859, Roll 49, Document 15635, National Archives.
Angell was Colonel of the Second Rhode Island Regiment. Whitmarsh's resignation
was accepted and effective on April 25, 1778.

John Chaloner to John Ladd Howell

Sir,   Commissarys Office March 9th, 1778
      Yours of the 5th, was this Moment handed to me, am glad to hear
of your success in procuring supplies, I must urge you to do all in your
power to forward every Barrel of flour to Camp you can possibly
procure teams to haul; I had hopes of sending a Brigade or two, but the
execution of the Law of this State, for that purpose is so relax, that I
have my fears of obtaining a sufficiency to haul the Necessary supplies,
as fast as wanted—do try to get a Brigade or two raised for that purpose,
for we now are without one Barrel of flour—I am—Sir Yours & ca

Source: Stewart Mss. 58.8, Rowan University Library.
This was addressed to Howell at Middletown, New Castle County, Delaware.

**Extract of a letter from a Gentleman at Camp at the
Valley Forge, dated March 9, 1778**

I am happy to inform you, that the southern states are pursuing the
most vigorous measures for strengthening the hands of General
Washington the ensuing campaign. Virginia has drafted 2000 men to
recruit her regiments, who are to serve for one year. They have also
set on foot an association for raising 5000 volunteers, to serve six
months. North-Carolina is exerting herself with equal ardor. The
eastern states, who in publick concerns always act with a wisdom and
vigor that deserves imitation, have already began to draft, being
resolved to fill their regiments completely, and to have them early in
the field. If the middle states take the same resolute steps, (and no
doubt they will) I think the next campaign must be decisive. The
strength of the enemy is so much reduced, that nothing but our
indolence can prevent their destruction.

I have often thought it strange that America, who could bring three or four hundred thousand men into the field, should so long suffer a paltry banditti to run through the state and to nestle in her cities. One would be tempted to imagine, that we were fond of this destructive war; and yet folly in her highest protraction and delay were prudent—even necessary; but at this time of day they will certainly be injurious, and may be fatal. Every day the war continues, our publick debts will increase—our necessities will multiply—our currency will depreciate. Britain knows this—she founds her last hopes upon it—she no longer expects to conquer us by the sword; but she flatters herself that our distresses will subdue our minds, break the spirit of our opposition, and dissolve in time the glorious confederacy in support of freedom. Hence it will be the policy of her generals to possess themselves our our towns, to destroy our manufactures, to block up our harbours, and to protract the war. We should change our measures accordingly—bring our thousands into the field—push the enemy with vigor—drive them from our towns—storms them in their strong holds, and never pause until we force them from our shores— The successes of the last campaign teach us what we are able to do if we exert our strength; and instead of provoking our indolence, should spur our ambition—These rising states should catch the spirit of the gallant Caesar, and think 'that they have done nothing, while any thing remains to do.'

Source: *The New Jersey Gazette* (Trenton), March 18, 1778.

David Kilgore to George Washington

To His Excellency George Washington Esqr.   March 10th. 1778.
Commander in Chief of the American Forces
The Petition of Captn. David Kilgore
Sheweth
That, Your Petitioner had the Honor to be appointed a Captain in the 8th. Pennsylvania Regiment, but finding it most inconvenient, as he has a large Family on the Western Frontier, who are now exposed to the mercy of the Savage Enemy, who have lately committed several ravages within a few Miles of Your Petitioners Plantation. He therefore begs Your Excellency's permission to Resign, as he may thereby be enabled to assist his distress'd family, should the Indians make any further

progress in that Country. Should Your Petitioner be so happy as to obtain that favour Your Petitioner as in duty bound shall ever Pray.

Sir   Camp
    I do certify that Captn. Kilgore is not indebted to the Reg^t. to the best of my knowledge—
                                                Daniel Brodhead
                                                Col. 8th Pens^a. Reg^t.
To his Excellency Genl. Washington

Source: RG 93, M859, Roll 110, doc, 31365, National Archives.
Kilgore was a Captain in the Eighth Pennsylvania Regiment. His resignation was accepted on March 12.

Jedediah Huntington to Jabez Huntington

Hon^d. Sir—   Valley Forge 13th. March 1778
                This comes by General Sullivan who is going to take Command at Providence—he is a very valuable Officer notwith standing some have attempted to injure his Character—
        General Greene is appointed Quarter Master General—who will, I am confident, soon put that Department in a respectable Condition—
        Capt Barry with some continental Soldiers on armed Boats in the Delaware has taken an armed Vessell of the Enemies and two Transports from Rhode Island loaded chiefly with Hay—the two latter he burn't the other he was obliged to abandon after taking out his Guns and other valuable Articles as he was hard push'd by several Frigates and other Vessels of force—The Conference of the Subject of a general Exchange of Prisoners is postponed to the last of this Month for urgent Reasons—
        Among the Letters on Board Capt Barrys Prize is one, mentioning the Embarkation of three hundred foreign Troops the 19th Decr. bound for Nyork—when they come, it is probably we shall have it announced in their Papers that as many thousand have arrived, several of these Letters which are from the Hessian Officers in NYork to their Friends in Philadelphia mention it as the Opinion of many, and their own hearty wish, that a peace would soon take place—
        I hope every Nerve will be exerted to render our Army formidable—we could not hardly wish Genl Howe in a more convenient

Situation to attack than he is now in, had we but our Complement of Troops, if every State had done like Connecticut, he would in all probability shared the Fate of Genl Burgoine long before this—

affectionate Remembrances to Mama and all friends conclude me your affect^e Son

Source: Huntington Papers, Connecticut Historical Society.

William Russell to Congress

Honorable Gentlemen,   [March 13, 1778]
    The Officers of that part of the 13th. Virginia Regiment that is now here, have desired me to state their present situation to you, and to request your serious attention to a matter not only of consequence to themselves but to the country at large. The present situation of our Frontiers, where most of the Regiment were raised, is precarious and alarming: under perpetual apprehensions from the neighboring savages, the inhabitants are obliged to crowd into forts, or withdraw themselves altogether from their settlements. Ruin and distress inevitably follow, and the most diligent and exertions of the heads of families are necessary to preserve them. In such circumstances the Officers conceive there is every reason to induce your honorable board to direct their march to that part of the country, where private as well as public interest are so strongly united to stimulate the most vigorous exertions against then own and their countrys enemies. But there are other arguments still stronger that might be urged. It seems agreed on all hands, and it wood be absurd to suppose otherwise, that the force now at Fort Pitt is absolutely necessary, and indeed insufficient for the defence of that important barrier. Part of the Regiment is left there; and the greater part torne from their distressed families, were ordered to join the Army, notwithstanding the assurances they had received that they should be stationed there.
The consequence followed which all might forsee, that they grew exceedingly uneasy on account of their connexions, distressed their officers with petitions, which, altho reasonable they could not grant, and at length finding all applications useless and flattering themselves with that forgiveness which they afterwards met, by joining that part of the Regiment at Fort Pitt they deserted largely and out of three hundred men I marched down in July, by the last return there were

only seventeen men present fit for duty. it was natural to expect that when a large part of the Regiment was left over the mountains, that the remainder both officers and soldiers wood be anxious to join them. Whoever has been in service will know how exceedingly disagreeable is the division of Regiments into detached bodies.

Officers lose a relish for the Service when their command dwindles into a handful of men, and it becomes utterly impossible to instruct them in military movements, or the discipline of a regular Army. What make it still more disagreeable is, that not only the Regiment, but every company in it is divided, except one and that is over the mountains.

Thus it is impossible to prevent desertions from this part of the Regiment to that. Colo. Gibson has the direction of that, and Major Campbell, nine Captains and my selfe have the command of the handfull here. But Colo Gibson has long been entitled to a regiment, and must soon join it, and then the disposal of the officers and the regiment will be still more absurd, as there will be no field Officer with the main body at Fort Pitt, and all the field Officers and a very great superabundance of the others to the part down with the Army. In short, I would beg leave to represent to your Honors, that there is no place where the 13th Virginia Regiment can be stationed with so much advantage as on the other side the Allegany. If they stay there, the regiment will be full and the men contented, as long as public and private interested coincide together. If they are sent down the country, their apprehensions for their families will occasion desertions and at any rate frequent applications for furloughs. But if they are divided, the part stationed here will be forever undone, as their interests are entirely against their stay, and the tie resulting from the union of men in Companies and Companies in a regiment becomes dissolved, and it will be impossible to keep them with any kind of content in the service.

I conceive there matters will be worthy your careful attention, as men are more wanting then Arms. If we do not shew attention to their reasonable desires, but sacrifice them to present occasions without looking forward to future contingencies, we may soon lament our unhappy inattention, and perhaps be exposed to the triumps of our enemies. I would therefore beg leave to conclude with the two following requests, either that the small part of the regiment now so unhappily situated here, be immediately ordered to the neighborhood of Fort Pitt, or if that most desirable request cannot be obtained, that then the whole regiment be drawn together and no longer continued in their present detachment situation. I have the honor to be, Gentlemen, with the greatest respect, your Most Obed. Servt.

Source: RG 360, Papers of the Continental Congress, M 247, Roll 101, i78 v19, p227, National Archives. Russell was Colonel of the Thirteenth Virginia. On May 24 Washington ordered the Valley Forge based part of the regiment to York, Pennsylvania, to await orders from Congress, they were eventually sent on to Fort Pitt.

Richard Kidder Meade to Lott Brewster

Sir   Head Quarters 14 March 1778
        Agreeable to my promise I informed His Exc^y. of your determination to resign your Commission, and expected to have found you in the House, and given you his answer verbally, but that not being the case, I take this method of communicating the Gen^{ls}. answer to you, which is as follows.—That the reduction of your Reg^{ts}. or as least the stay of the officers who Command them being a voluntary act, and all those officers necessary to be present, with their respective Reg^{ts}. He will not consent to your going without very sufficient reasons and those too are to be given in writing. I am &^{c}

Source: George Washington Papers, Roll 47, Library of Congress.
Meade was an Aide-de-Camp to Washington. Brewster, Colonel of the Third North Carolina Regiment, was allowed to resign on March 15, 1778.

Elias Boudinot to Elisha Boudinot

My Dr Brother   Camp March 15th 1778
        I wrote you a few days since, begging that you would do your Endeavours to procure me one of Gaines News Papers, in which is contained, an advertisement of the Sale of our money in reams which was counterfeited in New York—I also am in want of some Affidavits of the Treatment of our Prisoners in New York during the winter of 76 & 77, and the State of those who were sent out from New York the same Winter, about whom the dispite has subsisted between the two Generals—If you can find any Person of Credentials with you, I wish you would not loose a Moment in transmitting them to me—I have

been prevailed upon by the Generals sugestion, (much ag^t. my Will) to accept of the Place of one of the Commissioners for settling the Treaty of Exchange of Prisoners between the United States & General Howe as Head of the british Army—we are to set on the 31st. Ins^t. at German town—There are several Affidavits at Home, among my Papers in the black Trunk, I wish they could be forwarded without delay—

Not a line of News—We have a severe Time of it, nothing but suffering for our poor fellows, but they do it without Complaint—It has been severe weather for naked Soldiers—3000 of whom are down with the small Pox—not one lost by Innoculation out of this Number—

Am with kind love to M^{rs}. Burnet & family My Dr Brother yours very Affect^{ly}

Source: Thomas Addis Emmet Collection, #246, Manuscripts And Archives Division, New York Public Library.
Inoculation for smallpox was much more difficult for the adult patient than present day vaccination. The successful inoculation of 4,000 or so soldiers for smallpox, with only a handful of deaths, was a significant achievement of the Encampment.

William Bradford Jr. to Tacy Wallace

My dear Tacy,   Camp. March 15th 1778.

I received your letter a few days ago—I need not tell you how much pleasure this testimony of your affection gave me—your own heart can inform you. The articles you mention came safe to hand. Thank my dear Mamma for me—her kindness & attention deserves many thanks.—I have also the receipt of Master Joshua's to acknowledge—Tell the young Gentleman, that he is perfectly in the right—his nose is not out of joint yet—and it will be his own fault if it ever is so.

The best news I have to send you is that the southern & Eastern States are exerting themselves to the utmost to send a formidable force into the field early in the Campaign. Pennsylvania instead of adopting their vigorous mode of drafting is trying the old method of recruiting & offering the extravagant bounty of 120 Dollars, As this must occasion a new Emission of money, it has a destructive tendency & I hope will be laid aside. It is expected however, whether this state does her duty or not, that we shall have a large army in the field before the end of May which perhaps will be time enough to open the Campaign. I have no doubt we shall be an overmatch for the Enemy if they come out to meet us, & shall be able to drive them from Philad[a] whether they risk a battle or not—

This state still teems with Traitors who are continually attempting to supply the Enemy with Provisions. A few days ago four large Waggons loaded with flour & pork, which had been purchased in York Town & sent off towards Philad[a] for the use of the Enemy: fell in with Col. Morgan's Corps near the lines & who made a prize of them all. I hope the purchasers will be properly paid for their trouble.

You mention four shirts which you were mending for me— You will keep them till I write for them, as I have some hopes of being supplied here—I am anxious for the time when my business will indulge me with a Visit to Ellerslie. I count the days as they pass and am almost tempted like the poets "to chide their delay & bid them speed their flight." I flattered myself that I should have the pleasure of seeing you early in April. Col. Ward's departure to New England will prevent me—During his absence the burden of superintending the Department will rest on me & therefore it is probable I cannot obtain a furlow till his return which will be in May.

With regard to the pad, if it can be conveniently made at Rariton it will be best—

Give my kindest love to Mamma & remember me to all the family—I shall write to M[r] Wallace in a few days—Tommy & his family are well.

Adieu to my dear sister—Affectionately remember your own

Source: Selections From the Wallace Papers," *The Pennsylvania Magazine of History and Biography* 40 (1916): 338-39.
Despite the hopeful remarks by Bradford and others, on the vigorous recruiting efforts by the various states, many of the Continental Army regiments never approached their full complements of soldiers.

John Chaloner to Henry Champion

Commissaries Office Camp Valley forge

Sir   March 17th 1778

In the absence of Col[o]. Blaine your Letter of the 5th. Instant, was handed to me, wherein you appear to be anxiously concern'd for the difficulties with which you are embarress'd, by the immediate opperation of the regulating act. I embraced the earliest opportunity of laying the same before the Committee of Congress, now sitting here; The president of which was pleased to say that they had seen a Letter of the like nature to His Excellency the Commander in Chief, and as you had wrote Congress, he had no doubt but they would do the needful on this occasion & advised you thereof—

I heartily thank you for the Cattle you have already furnish'd us, and earnestly solicit you to continue your supplies & if possible to increase the number. 160 p^r Week now the Army is reduced & divided in Winter Quarters, have sufficed, but as Recruits are daily coming in, & in a very short period, the whole force of our Army will be collected here, must advise you very soon, nay immediately if in your power, to enlarge the Number—

If they are more than what is necessary for immediate Consumption, it will be easy to Salt them, which will preserve the Meat, without loss of Quantity or Quality—

You doubtless have seen His Excellencys address to the inhabitants of Maryland, Pennsylvania & W. Jersey, calling on them to prepare all the Beef Cattle they possible can for the Spring of the Year, & notwithstanding, his very pressing & earnest Solicitation on this occasion, I do not expect to reap any very material advantages therefrom.—These States having already supported both Armies for two Years, it is not in their power to do much now!—

You observe that you have Rec^d. no particular directions from Col. Blaine, with regard to the Quantity or posts to send to; In answer to which must inform you, that the Quantity must not be less if possible than 200 head per Week, and the Grand army the only post we are most anxious to supply—in a word, the Quantity cannot be too great, nor too soon forwarded—Confident of your combating every difficulty & embarrassments that may oppose or obstruct, with the Vigour, exertion and Perseverance necessary to insure success—& afford that needful supply—I Remain Sir Your most Obed^t hble Servant

Source: Mss. 69492, Connecticut Historical Society.
Champion was a Deputy Commissary General of Purchases at Hartford, Connecticut. The difficulties of driving two hundred cattle a week from Connecticut to Valley Forge on unpaved roads, and crossing unbridged major rivers such as the Hudson and Delaware, can only be imagined.

Robert Hanson Harrison to Elias Boudinot

D^r. Sir   March 17, 1778
   I am sorry to hear you are indisposed and hope you will soon
recover. I have never dabbled much in Medical authors or given great
credit to the tales of Old Women, and therefore hold myself but illy
qualified to prescribe for any malady: However I will hazard my
reputation for once. put a Woollen Stocking round your neck to night
& it is more than probable you will derive no small benefit from it. I
have myself in a complaint of a similar nature.
   As to the Hessian & British Officers, who have come to
Lancaster, the General thinks you had better send them in on parole.
He desires you will have a particular list taken of their names-ranks &
Corps & set against their names such of our Officers of equal rank; as
should be permitted the same indulgence in return for them; a Copy of
which you will transmit Mr Ferguson with a requisition for an order
to have ours liberated—The General also desires that the Officers
may be conducted by a proper route, that they may avoid this Camp,
and under the Escort of a discreet Officer from Lancaster, who will
attend them as far as their Lines.
   In a Letter from Genl Howe which came to hand last night on
the subject of an Exchange between Lt Cols Allen & Campbell—he
says he always understood Mr Allen was a Colo—do inform me
Whether the List you have mentioning Allen to be a Lt Colo, is signed
by Mr Loring or by whom—I should also be glad if you could mention
the names of the French Officers who were received by the Enemy
last Winter and under what rank in the first instance & how it was
changed. We must write Sir William immediately concerning our
Friend Allen. He is angry that we should have expressed any
suspicions as to his intentions respecting General Lee—but you might
as well expect to find generosity in a Jew or virtue in the British
Parliament, as to expect him to make an explicit Declaration, that
Genl Lee is like other prisoners & on the same footing he has
acknowledged it & he shall confess his right of an exchange before
we are done with him. Adieu Yrs Affy

Source: Elias Boudinot Papers, Mss. Division, Library of Congress.
Harrison was Military Secretary to George Washington. The Mr. Allen referred to
was Ethan Allen of Vermont, who was exchanged in May.

Alexander Scammell to Timothy Pickering

Dear Sir,   Camp Valley Forge March 17^tnth 78.
I have now sit down to fulfill my promise of writing a long Letter, if
these milk & water, white livered, unsancify'd Quakers don't
interrupt me in Behalf of their Friend in Y^e provost. I am
apprehensive that I shall imbibe an inveterate Hatred against the
whole sect, or rather against those who make a Cloak of that
profession to perpetrate the blackest Villainies. You will perhaps hear
of one Worrells being condemn'd, & sent to Bucks County & hung in
Terrorem Toryorum. Numbers of those Villains are continually in our
house of Jereboam, which the other night was set on Fire by them, in
order to escape by the light of it, but happily didnot effect their
purpose. Nothing but the Terrors of Death, and frequent Execution of
some of them, can have the least Effect upon them and that wont stop
their insatiable avarice of Gold for which they would sacrifice their
all, nay sell their God, for a Less price than Judas. Some of Morgan's
Corps made a fine Hawl upon a Tory from near York Town who had
arriv'd within a mile of the enemy's Lines when the Riflemen under
Lt Harden attack'd them, the Horses being exceeding smart push'd
over, & evaded the footmen, when Harden alone persued them;
attack'd six of them, kill'd one, and took 4 fine Waggons loaded with
flower, & Forrage—drawn by four excellent Horses each with a Chest
of Cloathing, &^c. The Villain who own'd them by means of a spry
Horse made his Escape. Two of the drivers were brought in—The
whole Booty is estimated at 3000£. So it seems you have some
disaffected Inhabitants near the Senate—Even at your Door. It is a
lucky Circumstance that the Waggons didn't reach the City as it must
have been a Reflection upon our army to suffer so much to pass to the
enemy—It is an unpardonable Crime in the unprincipled Inhabitants
of this State that they have supply'd a Number greater then our whole
army with provisions, contrary to every Law human & divine, whilst
our brave Soldiery have been perishing for want of necessaries,
although risquing their Lives in Defence of those very parricides,
Liberty & property. It is too much for a man of principle to bear with
any degree of patience. I am sometimes for slaying all before me, and
effectually eradicate a set of wretches whom the Earth must grown
[*sic*] under their Burthen—Again I shudder at the prospect, when I see
Citizens hawl'd before Courts martial, hung, whip'd & robbed by the
military power and hear their wives & Children weaping & bewailing

their friends punishment; till I turn my Reflections upon the mourning Widows, helpless Orphans, & fields of the crimson Gore of our Friends, Brothers, & Countrymen sacrificed, reduced to misery, and a melancholly Life in defence of our Cause, & Country, occasion'd by such miscreants—My Indignation again overflows & such interesting reflections calls up every tender Idea of our struggling Country's miseries—Making the disaffected inimical Inhabitants amenable to martial Law has occasion'd much Trouble and business in addition to the multiplicity that ever will be in our Army, more especially in this Office—But cant see how it can be avoided under the present relax'd Government of this State—

You mention'd the several Obstructions and Hindrances to making our Opperations go on with Vigor as they ought to do to give any probable assurance of Success, I am very unhappy to hear it—But one thing above all I am fearful of, Viz that the new Arrangement will create uneasiness in the army as the N$^{\underline{o}}$ of Officers are to be reduc'd, and I am apprehensive their pay no more respectable—What has kept the greater part of our Officers in Camp this Winter was the Expectation that they would be put upon the half pay Establishment, if that is not the Case, you may depend upon it, so far as I know the minds of the Officers; who remain will be uneasy at the time when we ought to push on with Vigour & every Officer ambitious to do his best, animated not only with the goodness of the Cause, but with a prospect of not being reduc'd to Beggary at the end of the War or his family left in want—The Idea of half pay I dont imagine would ever have enter'd their minds had not they experience'd the severities of several Campaigns, and the avariciousness of their Neighbour's who have most inhumanly permitted their wives & Families to suffer & almost perish at home whilst they were risquing their Lives for the good of the whole. There is no Competition to be put between Life & property, & I think we cant give too great Encouragement to those brave men who experience the severeties of a Camp Life, and chearfully expose their Lives with a determination to die or conquer. No Expences should be stuck at, to give every opperation Life & Vigor, and encourage the best of men to enter and continue in the Service—which can never be done, so long as people enjoying domestick Ease are making their Fortunes, whilst those in ye field are spending theirs, unless Commissions are made more profitable and worth seeking for, in common estimation; For you are sensible that the Virtue among the americans is not sufficient at present, to influence them to remain & act in the army for the good of the Cause, & honor only unless back'd & seconded by the Idea of profit—Unless our Virtue & Patriotism should encrease at home, where the Example ought to be set—It may be objected to, that by putting the Officers upon the half pay Establishment, much public money would be paid to unworthy Officers—& when the war is over a considerable Expence would be entail'd upon the States—But we must at the same time reflect that we had better pay a few unworthy Officers (who may be dis[ ]'d occasionally) than risque the Loosing of great part of our good Officers—And as to the entail expence it will be but trifling compar'd with the good Consequences it will more immediately produce. The Idea at present entertain'd of Commissions is so low That many of our Officers would be glad of an Opportunity to git rid of them—knowing that if even they should be cashier'd they shall be able at home to make more money & do better for themselves, & Families there, than in the army. What is it makes the british Officers so much superior to ours, but the Value of their Commissions, their consciousness of Dependence upon them for a Livelihood & their ambitious Views to excell in their Calling or rather Trade, if I may be allow'd the expression—They gratefully look up to the King as their patron, Benefactor, & Fountain of Honor, & that they are under the highest Obligations to him; & in Duty bound to exert every abolity in grateful Acknowledgement to their Sovereign—Thus good Officers make good men an invariable maxim in the Art of war—Whilst it is quite the reverse with us—The Officers of our army look upon it that the Country the Congress, are obligated, that they are under no greater Obligation than to fight, than their Neighbours that they shall shortly retire home, to domestick ease and let others take their places, therefore they think it not worth their while to perfect themselves in the art of war, and endeavor to shine in their present Stations as the fear of loosing their commisions diminishes, their Carelissness of Duty increases—their Thoughts are fixed too much, upon their domestick Employments to give proper attention to military Discipline—If Congress will put them upon an honorable and profitable (I contemn & despise any thing that sounds of self Interest.) they will think themselves obligated more strictly to their Duty; and be lead by Interest & Duty, which opperate most cogently upon the human Breast. They will esteem themselves generously used by their Countrymen which will in great measure remove their Cause of Complaint against those at whom [sic] engaged in accumulating wealth. The half pay establishment will give them surpprizing spirit & influence them to discipline their men more carefully be more attentive to learn, & do their Duty, be more anxious to defeat the enemy in order the sooner to reap the Fruits of their Toil & Fatigues, in domestick Felicity, & perhaps thereby save the States the expence of several Campaigns, which will save more than the Expence of half pay, should the Officers vie with Methuselah in point of Legevity. Besides as we have the best of men, if we had the best of Officers, of consequence we should have the best army in the world—Our Officers are young, and should have something extraordinary to encourage them to undefatigable Application in learning the Duty of their profession. Our Cause may be properly, & very justly urged, as the best motive in the world, but previous to our Independency, our manners Had become so much tainted by the Examples of our step dame, that Self Interest, that hateful, tho all prevailing motive in the hearts of mankind in Genl must be gratify'd in some measure, more especially where depravity of manners, vice & Luxury has gain'd ground—We were once look'd upon, as the most virtuous people in the world, would to God the assertion could be now made consistent with Veracity—But as avarice has crept in at home to so great a Degree that our Officers Families must be vastly oppress'd and suffer many cruel Inconveniencies if not want and the bare necessaries of Life, whilst they are perhaps ruining their Constitutions in the army— These considerations must shock the most rigid patriotism, Whey they reflect, that they may at the end of the war, be renderd unfit to gain a Livelihood or retrieve their Estates expended, or very much diminish'd by being in the Service—Whilst their Neighbours have sav'd their Constitutions, augmented their Estates, and equally share the benefit of their Valor and exertions in repelling Tyranny, & freeing their Country—Unless their Country generously make provisions for them, and put them upon half pay Establishment—The Officers are in high Expectation of it, and should they find themselves disappointed, a general Dissolution of the Officers I am almost sure, will take place—which at this important Crisis, may produce the most fatal Consequences, as we ought immediately to open the Campaign.

 I am in hopes that a stop is put to Desertions in our army in a great measure, as the enemy put those who desert from us on board Ships & transport them to some of their Fortresses in the east, or west Indies, to prevent their Deserting & relieve Soldiers in those Garrisons, whom they can depend upon—As the british Soldiery seems to be much disaffected I am certain if we took pains by certain emisaries to give them proper information, and encouragement, in fact only to convince them of the Treatment they receive whilst with us, many more of them would come over than now do—Their officers ever exerting themselves to keep the Soldiery in Ignorance—If an address containing a promise of good usage, and certifying what bounty they should receive and pay for their Arms; should be drawn up printed & sent into Philadelphia to be dispers'd amongst the Soldiery, I presume it would draw off many of them.

I have urg'd the Genl Officers several times the necessity of having our Officers begin upon discipline immediately, of having one Officer from each Brigade order'd to assemble at a particular place to settle one uniform plan or mode, which they should teach and communicate to all the Officers of their Brigades respectively—& by that means have the Officers renderd capable of teaching their men all in the same manner—I hope something will be done that way soon, otherwise our Officers will be poorly able to do their duty, in a general way, and our troops badly disciplind—I have urg'd the Committee of Congress to use their Influence in procuring Liberty for me to get a Band of music establish'd, and the Expence defray'd and included in the contingent Bill—the Band to be under my Eye, and to attend the parade every Day, attend reviews, and other public Occasions—hope it will be granted—As I am certain it will be exceeding serviceable and the profit be much greater than the Cost— & The utile & dulee be advantageously blended—The gloomy Idea of Famine is in a great measure dissipated at present by a good supply of provisions in Camp—I understand the State of Connecticut only has 10,000 head of Cattle stall feeding for the army—One of the Frigates has escap'd out of Providence River, & put to sea. [Some] complements of men are already drafted, as I am informd in New England to fill our Reg^{ts} hope they'll soon arrive—A very good prospect that Government will be soon establish'd if it has energy sufficient to draft men at this early period which is with difficulty performd in old, well regulated States—Excuse the Length of this Letter, out of the fulness of the heart the mouth speaks, Y^r Friend & Servt.

Source: Timothy Pickering Papers, Massachusetts Historical Society.
Scammell's diatribe expresses the anger many men felt against the Quakers, and other citizens of Pennsylvania, who were believed to be actively supporting the

British Army in Philadelphia. The issue of half pay for officers was a contention of many, including Washington, that without the incentive of such a measure, good officers would continue to resign. On May 27, Congress did pass a resolution granting officers who continued to the end of the war, half pay for seven years.

Benjamin Tupper to Henry Laurens

Sir,   Camps near Valley Forge, March 19th 1778

On or about the 20th of Octob^r. A:D: 1775 His Excellency Genl. Washington being inform'd that two Vessells Viz^t. a Brigantine of about 175 Tun and a Sloop of ab^t. Belonging to Benjⁿ. Mulberry Holmes, W^m. Taylor and Nathl. Coffin of Boston (the Former then in Arms against the United States, the two Latter Notorious Enemies to their Country, both having since gone off with the Enemy) had arrived at Marthas Vineyard from a Whaling Voyage, & as the Vineyard Sound was under the power of the Enemy, to prevent said Vessells being sent to Boston: His Excellency was pleased to give me Special orders to proceed to the Vineyard and Seize said Vessells with their Cargoes and secure them in Some Safe port on the Continent for the Benefit of the States—

I proceeded to in Consequence of his Orders, & hired armed men, crost the sound, took Possession of said Vessells, Cargo's &c. & carried them into Bedford in Dartmouth & according to Orders deliver'd the whole to the Care of W^m. Watson Esqr. Continental Agent at Plymouth who found some difficulty in Libelling said Vessells &c. on Acc^t. of their not being bound to Boston to Supply the Enemy with Provisions &c; and as there was some doubt whether the Captures were included in the Limits of any resolve of Congress, prior to that Time; the Trial of them has been Suspended and the Vessells are not Sold (Except Lately) and as the Vessells were Excellent good Sailors & might be of Service to the Continent if properly attended to, I humbly take the Liberty to represent the matter to your Honor that if it's Thought best that they may be disposed off; for if they be much Longer unoccupied they will be Inevitably ruined.—The owners had sent to have the Vessells convey'd to Boston, But the Hands which had been in them refused to go there But as the Sound was Continually occupied by the Enemy's Ships & Arm'd Vessells no doubt they would soon have found means to have taken them, and as I not only run a risk in going after them, as great as was Common in, Attempting to Take Vessells at that day but was also at a great deal of Extra Cost and pains about the Attempt; for which I never recd^d, any gratuity, I cant but think I am justly intitled to a share of them.—If your Honor would be pleased to proposed to the Honble. Congress to have them Subject to a Trial like other Captures or otherwise as in your Wisdom shall seem meet: so that the Vessells be prevented from further destruction, and that I might meet with some reward for my extra Service: you will greatly oblige, Your Honor's Most Obedient, Humble Servant.

Source: RG 360, Papers of the Continental Congress, M 247, Roll 103, i78, v32, p557-59, National Archives.
Tupper was Colonel of the Eleventh Massachusetts Regiment.

David Grier to William McPherson

Dear Sir,   Camp Near Schuylkill 20th March 1778
I was at Marsh Creek lately & there saw your two Letters Requesting that some hard Money be sent you I have now delivered the Commissary of Prisoners with this letter five half Johannes which I hope will be sufficient untill you are released. should it not be sufficient Write me by the first Oppertunity I suppose you have heard e're this your Sister Janny has in a frenzy fit Married a Soldier, & Exchanged the name of McPherson for that of Grier: Please to Remember me to Maj: Bailey tell him I saw M^{rs}: Bailey four Days since they were all well & in high Expectations of seeing him soon: I hope to have the Pleasure of your Company soon as a Genl. Exchange is soon Expected. your father Mother Sisters & Brothers all desire to be remembered to you. Excuse haste & believe me Esteem yours sincerely

Source: Mss Division, William McPherson Mss., Library of Congress.
Grier was Lt. Col. of the Seventh Pennsylvania Regiment. McPherson was a Lieutenant in Miles' Pennsylvania Rifle Regiment, who was a prisoner of war at Flat Bush, Long Island. He was exchanged a month later and resumed service.

Elias Boudinot to Elisha Boudinot

My D^r. Brother   Camp March 21st. 1778
    Major Burnet was here the night before last and told me some

confused Story about you keeping some Liquors for me as Commissary of Prisoners—I cannot concieve what it means, as I know of no Liquors I spoke to you about, and he can tell me neither Head or Tail about it—He says I must send you a Certificate about them, I therefore altho' entirely in the dark enclose something at a Venture, which you must destroy if of no use—I am amazed you could not have wrote a Line by him, for confusion will allways attend Business done in so useless a manner—I expect to be at Germantown on the 31st. and as soon as that Business is over, intend to resign and leave the Army—But apropos, you have now an Opportunity to show your Zeal & Courage for the Common Cause—

The Congress have solemnly called on all the Young Gent^n of fortune & Courage to form themselves into Troops of Horse, to choose their own Officers, & to turn out to join the Army till the 1st. of Decr. Gratis—They are to be found Provision & Ammunition—They are not to be used in Expresses nor to be on any Guard but the Generals & & & Now if you are of a Mind to make your fortune & raise your Character, turn out—Each Troop from a State is to be called after the State, and to have all the Plunder divided between them—

I have been confined with a slight Quincey for a few days, but thank a kind & generous God, am ready to turn out again the first good day—Am in great Haste Yours Affect^y.

I wish an Answer to my last two letters lately wrote—

Source: Thorne-Boudinot Letters, Princeton University Library.

Friedrich Wilhelm Augustus von Steuben to Horatio Gates

Honorable Sir   Camp Valley Forge March ye 21th. 1778

I Should not have delayed So long to have the honor to Write to Your Excellency, had I not been Waiting Every Day for Something Worth the While to acquaint you With: But, Now that I have the best News to impart you, you could not but accuse me With forgetfulness or neglect, if I stood one Day longer without performing So agreeable a Duty.—I have met with the most favorable Reception from all the Generals in your Army, and Genl Washington in particular. His Excellency is willing to Entrust me with the Department of the Exercising and Discipline of the Troops. In order to perform so hard a

Task, I shall Want extremely the Counsels of Experienced Generals Such as your Actions have Shewn you to be, and I shall think myself very happy, if you will honor me with yours—I dare hope you will not refuse me what Shall lay your Country as well as myself under the greatest Obligation to Your Excellency. Mr defrancy has acquainted me with your being always in good health, I wish you may long continue So, as well as your Lady, whom I take the Liberty to assure of the respect with which I have the honor to be Honorable Sir your Excellency's most obedient and most humble servant

Source: The Horatio Gates Papers, Manuscript Department, The New-York Historical Society. At this time Steuben held no official post. He soon proved himself in training the troops and in May, based on Washington's enthusiastic recommendation, Congress appointed him Inspector General with the rank of Major General. Major General Gates was then President of the Board of War, meeting in York, Pennsylvania.

Elias Boudinot to Elizabeth Ferguson

My Dear Madam,   Valley Forge, March 24, 1778.

Your favour by Major West came to hand this morning, and as he has promised me to call at my Quarters to morrow morning, I hope to have the pleasure of conveying this by him on his return. I hope you do not even suspect me of passing you on any occasion, without at least asking how you do? When I returned from Jersey, I was informed that the Enemy was in your Neighbourhood, having just taken off a drove of our Cattle; wherefore I was obliged to pass several miles above Corryell's ferry and came down on the rear of our Camp. I intended have honored myself by taking shelter for one night more under your hospitable Roof; and in consequence was the bearer of two Letters for you from Morven, which were not to be delivered but by myself. In this however, you have heard of my misfortune, in being deprived of that Pleasure.

I am happy in enclosing you £106.4.0 in full for the Certificate of 2360 Pounds of Beef at 90/ p. ct., which I hope will get safe to your hands.

Your great attention to our unfortunate Countryman and fellow citizens demands the Thanks of every friend of humanity. As I am one of the Commissioners to sit at German Town next Wednesday, I think it would be best to collect the Linnen, and send it to me there; or rather I will endeavour to send for it to your House, where I hope to steal an Evening during our negotiation.

I have been confined to my Room with a slight Indisposition, but through the goodness of God am again able to go out. I do assure you a Camp in such a Wilderness is a horrid place to be sick in. It made me feel the loss of my humble Cot and dear family with double force. I pant eagerly after that domestic felicity of which I have allways been so large a partaker, and expect to take my leave of the Army in a few weeks, but whether I shall obtain my desires of sinking into my wished for obscurity, in the silent enjoyment of those invaluable Pleasures incompatible with publick Life, I know not; but rather hope for it, than think it will be affected.

My kindest Love and best wishes attend you with Miss Stedman, who I hope has not forgot her old Friend who I can assure her often thinks of her. I am Dr Madam, with great respect and Esteem Your Most Affect^e and very Hble Servt

Source: *Pennsylvania Magazine of History and Biography*, 39 (1915): 291-92.
Mrs. Ferguson's husband Hugh, was a Deputy Commissary of Prisoners with the British in Philadelphia. Her home of Graeme Park in Montgomery County, is a historic site administered by the Pennsylvania Historical and Museum Commission.

Henry Beekman Livingston to Robert R. Livingston

Dear Robt.   Camp Valley Forge 25th: March 1778
I rec^d: Your fav^r: of 20th: Feb^{ry}: some time Since and Should have wrote to You before But have for near Six Weeks been confined to my Bed in the Neighbourhood of Camp I would Aske a Furlough for the Purpose of Paying You a Visit did I not know the Request would give Pain to his Excellency which I would not willingly do—We have a Prussian Lieutenant-General (arrived in Camp) and Knight of the Black Eagle &c which he wears made of Lead Tied to one of his Button Holes he is taken great notice of and is Appointed Inspector-General of the Army he is now Teaching the Most Simple Parts of the Exercise such as Position and Marching of a Soldier in a Manner Quite different from that, they have been heretofore used to, In my Oppinion More agreable to the Dictates of Reason & Common Sence than any Mode I have before seen he is an agreable man about fifty five and talks English Pretty Well, French and German as far as I am

Capable of Judging very well, we are first Taught to March without Musick but the Time of March is given as Slow Time is a Medium between what was in Our service Slow and Quick Time Quick Time about as Quick as a Common Country Dance—I rec^d. no Letters by M^r: Lawrence—Am much Obliged to You for the Efforts used in my Fav^r: But am by no means sanguine in my Expectations I have not the least doubt but that I shall be Appointed to the Command of one of the light Infantry Corps to be drafted from the Army for the Purpose of Scirmishing In front But as it will be an Acquisition of Danger without the Most distant Prospect of Acquiring Honour adequate; I think it would be much Better for me to retire to my Little Farm But I have other Reasons which Impell me more forcibly not to mention my Fondness for retirement I am however determine to Continue here untill I have Learnt the New Dicipline as I would not Chuse to be Ignorant of it—The Letters of Mine &c that You Allude to Must have fallen into the hands of the Enemy with My Chest of Cloaths sent from Albany to the Manour By a Capt: Mott who Carried them to Poghkeepsie where I believe his Vessel Was Burnt the Letter sent Col^o. Biddle I cannot Account for I Approve of Your Caution—I Am Far from being of Your Opinion with resspect to the Northern Expedition which I believe You only disapprove of because Ignorant of the Design, which is to I believe only for the Purpose of Raising the Vessels Sunk by the Enemy in Lake Champlain which will give us a Superiority by Water in that Department and I believe undertaken on Certain Information that the Enemy had Abandoned their Posts on this Side Montriol and were retireing from that City—also an Assurance from the Canadians that they would take up Arms on the Appearance of our Troops North of Lake Champlain I am Just going to dine at Lord Stirlings—

27th. the Ladies are well as You will no doubt be Informed by the Packquets sent by the Bearer should be glad You would forward all the Letters I send as I am particularly Intrusted with them—I send jack Express that I may be Certain of Hearing from You and that I may be as soon as possible be enabled to pay a Debt Incurd to D^r: Vashe who I am now endeavouring to Breake for disobedience of Orders and Insolent behavior he has duned me for the Money Since his Arrest which makes Me the More Anxious the whole is seven Guineas and a Half hard Cash expended in Runing a Piece of Linnen Cambrick and some Stockings from Philadelphia which are now some time since arrived Safe Should be glad You Would Procure the

Money for me and send in by Jack also my Horse if he is fat if not Should be much Obliged to You if You would purchase for me a good Strong and Hansome Horse Price about £100"0"0 and put my Mare and Horse &c to Pasture for me on my Farm or Elsewhere Mama will furnish Money for the Purchase of a Horse for me let him be a Bay and fat if Possible—As there will be many Vacancies in my Reg^t. should be much Obliged to You if You would recommend to Govr: Clinton 8 Young Men of Capacity for Ensigns they are unfit if they do not read write a Legible Hand and understand Arithmetick, Theodorus V^n: Vycke Graham I recommend as one. I Am Acquainted with no one else who I would Wish to have provided for—The New Arrangement as settled by a Committee from Congress is as follows for a Reg^t:—

No New Col^o. to be Created as they have not the Avantage of Exchange

    1 L^t. Col^o.
    1 Major
    6 Captains
    1 Captain Lieutenant
    8 Lieutenants
    9 Ensigns

Adjudant and Q^r. Master & Pay Master to be taken from the Line According to this Arrangement and the Recommendations I have given I shall have Vacant In my Reg^t. 2 Lieutenants and Nine Ensigns. The Apointment of these are left to the State who I hope will improve the Service and not render it worse as they did in their last Appointments—I Am Dr Brother Yours Aff^{tly}

Source: Robert R. Livingston Papers, Manuscript Division, The New-York Historical Society. Livingston's comments are a tribute to the early effectiveness of Steuben's training. See the letter of Dr. "Vashy" dated April 6.

Richard Butler to Thomas Wharton Jr.

Sir   Camp Valley Forge, 26th. March 1778 It is with pain I sit down to address your Excellency at a time that I am Sencible your mind is taken up in the many Calls of Your Country that demand your Care & Particular Attention—but I think I should be wanting in the trust you have reposed in me, were I to neglect leting you know the wants of the Regt. I have the honr. to Command in the

Service of ye States; I find Sir that the men are good and Can be much depended on as brave Soldiers, and that nothing but their Naked Sittuation induces any of them to Leave me, the want of Cloathing is the first thing that makes A Soldier think little of himself, the want of Pay, & Provissions Irregularly serv'd. will make him Uneasy, but that is not the Case with these, (they are well paid & fed,) therefore I think had I Cloathing for them I would Venture to Vouch for their Conduct both as to their bravery & fidelity, and am Certain it would be very Conducive to their health. I am Sorry to Inform your Excellency that there has not been A blanket to five men through the whole winter, and the Chief of them but one Shirt, and many none, (Indeed I may almost say with Sir John Falstaff one & a half to A Compy.) this your Excellency may depend is the case, but I will do my Endeavour to keep them together, and nurse them as well as I Can, in hopes your Excellency and the Supreme Council will afford me Relief as soon as Possible, Shall hope the honor of a line on the Subject as it will give great weight to my Assertions of speedy Relief—I Remain With the Most Profound Respect Your Excellencys most Obedt. & very Humble Servt.

Source: RG 27, Roll 13, frame 1056, Pennsylvania Historical and Museum Commission. Butler was Colonel of the Ninth Pennsylvania Regiment.

John Cochran to the Committee of Congress at Camp

Gentlemen   Valley Forge Camp March 26th. 1778
    The Rev^d: Doctor David Jones Chaplain to the 5th. Pennsylvania Regiment, has done the Duty of Surgeon to the 4th. Pennsylvania Regiment, from the 10th. of July last, with great care and diligence, Therefore pray a resolve of Congress that, he may be continued to do the duty of Chaplain and Surgeon in the same manner as Doctor Griffith—There was no other Surgeon in pay during this Attendance on S^d Regiment—
    During the last Campaign and Winter several Regiments have had no surgeons, I consequently have been obliged to employ one or other of the Brigade Surgeons to attend the Sick of Said Regiments— Therefore pray a resolve of Congress for additional pay, on my giving Certificates of the Duty being performed—

Further, pray a Resolve of Congress, preventing Surgeons or Mates Serving in the Marching Regiments, from being promoted or employed in any of the General Hospitals unless regularly discharged from their respective regiments, by the Commander in Cheif or the Surgeon General of the Army, in the respective district to which he or they belongs—I have the honor to be Gentlemen Your very humble Servant

Source: RG 360, Papers of the Continental Congress, M 247, , Roll 57, i43, p119, National Archives. Cochran was Surgeon General for the Middle Department. Congress appointed Jones as Chaplain to the Second Pennsylvania Brigade on May 25, but he apparently did not act as Surgeon. See Wayne to Henry Laurens, May 13.

George Fleming to Sebastian Bauman

Dear Sir,   Camp, 26th March, 1778
    I wrote you a day or two ago a few Lines by Capt. Doughty, and then acknowledged the receipt of your agreeable Favor of the 7th Instant.
    I am inexpressibly Happy to find you approve of my being with General Du Portail;—he is, as I prognosticated, an exceeding affable, genteel Man; and seems to take pleasure in instructing me.—
    I return you ebullitions of Thanks for the favourable Sentiments, you were pleased to express, you retain of me. My Conduct shall never be such as to cause you to retract your good opinion.
    I have delivered to Lieut. How, conformable to your directions, the Papers that concern the Company. M^r. How has received your Decem^r. and Extraordinary Months Pay—which he has in his hands.
    Pray Remember me most Cordially to my old Friend & Neighbour Winant Van Zandt; tell him I heartily congratulate him on his Enlargement, Please to present my Compliments to his worthy Father, M^{rs}. & Miss Van Zandt.
    The Party you heard that were forming against a great Personage, consists only of Tories, a few that professed themselves Whigs that have embezzled the Publick Monies, and would do any thing to create confusion, and an over ambitious Man or two, who have made themselves dispicable by their Presumption & Vanity. "Them that make Envy and crooked Malice nourishment dare bite the best"—is what I

think some Poet said, but the Reports of Cannon have eradicated his name out of my head.

The Recruit I informed you, I had enlisted, and Deserted, was taken up near Lancaster by a Captain in the Pensy[la]. Line, for Deserting from him:—he is now in safe Custody.

I have got Rich[d]. Dikman to take care of our riding Horses until the General gets a Hostler, as he discharged his for Misdemeanor a few days since.—

You mention you would be glad to know how to direct to me—I am now Brigade Major Pro. Tem. which I sign to all my Writings by order of the General; whether that alters my Appellation or not I don't know—it is immaterial.

Luke Norestrant informs me, you expect to be here the latter end of this Month; I shall be happy in seeing you.

Sullivan's Bridge is finished. Deserters come in very fast from the Enemy. Nothing has transpired since Cap[t]. Doughty's departure. Cap[t]. Lee now commands the Eight Companies. Col[s]. Crane & Proctor are near at Daggers Points. We daily expect to see Gen[l]. Lee. Col[l]. Hamilton is so hurried that he has not yet had time to write to you.—He looks like Death!!! I remain with unfeigned Respect & Esteem Dear Sir, with most Respectful Compliments to M[rs]. Bauman & Family, Your Obed[t]. and Devoted Serv[t].

Source: Sebastian Bauman Papers, Manuscript Department, The New-York Historical Society.

Elias Boudinot to Hannah Boudinot

My Beloved Wife—   Camp March 27th. 1778
I have this Moment returned from a Consultation of two Days with my fellow Commissioners, and am made extremely happy by the receipt of your kind, tender & affectionate Letters by the Express, and altho' it is late and I am wearied with writing, yet I cannot help indulging myself with a Scrawl to my beloved & invaluable Wife, thanking her in the sincerity of my Heart for those soft Expression of Love & tenderness which could only be dictated by Affection and Esteem—

That the dear Object of my most passionate and fond desires, should entertain & cherish Sentiments so flattering to my Vanity, is full as much as I have a right to expect; and must yield a degree of Pleasure & Gratification, to be exceeded only by a personal Enjoyment of what you know I prize as the Chief of my earthly Happiness—May all the Blessings & Comforts of this World & the World to Come, which you wish for me, be showered down in a double Portion on my sweetest Wife & beloved Daughter—I expect to set off for German Town on Tuesday Morning, on the Business of our Commission. It is not very pleasing, as it is one of those Employments, that tho' we act upright as Angels, yet we are sure of not pleasing any one—The Expectations & Desires of Mankind (which regulate those Expectations) so far exceed the true mark, that we know that if we act justly, we shall meet the disapprobation of those who judge from so variable & unreasonable a rule—In this Business we shall endeavour to please ourselves by acting faithfully & uprightly, and to please our General by convincing him of the Principles on which we act, and leave all others to find fault, as they please, laying it to our Account, that if we come off without loosing our reputation altogether, we do better & shall be more favoured than many who have gone before us.

My dear Susan's Excuses are rather those of negligence & want of inclination, than those of necessity—Did she set apart one day in a Week to favour her Papa with a Letter, however short, I do not think it would be a great Sacrifice, seeing she is interested in the Event; but you know the old Proverb, "out of sight, out of mind." Kiss her for me, and give my kind Love to the family, Sisters friends & Neighbours—

We have intelligence in Camp that there is a great number of French Vessels (merch[t] men) under Convoy of a 50 Gun Ship arrived at the Carolina's—That our Vessels are admitted to formal Entr[ance] at the Custom House in Martinico and pay the usual Duties—That this has been the occasion of a remonstrance from the Gov[r] of Antigua, but to no Effect—

And now my dearest & most beloved of Women, I must with all the tenderness & Affection of the most loving Husband, wish you a good Night, with the addition of every Happiness your nature is capable of in this Vale of Tears & disappointments, and after they are vanished away like the baseless fabrick of a nocturnal Vision leaving not a [wrech] behind, you may find yourself in the full fruition of all the Joys & raptures of the most adoring Seraph of the heavenly World—

I do no more, than copy the real lineaments of my fond Heart, when I again & again assure you with fresh & repeated expressions of Esteem how much I thou dear Partner of all my Hopes, Joys and Expectations

The most tender & Affectionate of Husbands

Boudinot

P.S. I hope to seem you before I take any conclusive Measures relative to my future Conduct—
I rec^d the Papers & they contain what I wanted—
Lady Stirling, Lady Kitty & Miss Brown are well
M^{rs}. Washington often asks after you, she have given me your Cotton seed—

Source: Stimson Boudinot Collection, Princeton University Library.

Israel Angell to Luke Griffith

Camp Valley Forge, 30th March 1778

I engage to write as soon as convenient to Colo. Green now raising a Regt. of negros in the State of Rhode Island, respecting negrow Tone, the property of Mr. Luke Griffith of the State of Maryland) now serving in my Regt. as a soldier, properly enlisted, and if agreeable to his sentiments, to purchase and pay upon demand for sd negro tone whatever sum of money the State of Rhode Island allows for able bodied slaves. And to acquaint Mr. Griffith as soon as possible on receipt of an answer from Col° Greene, but if the contrary, to deliver up sd negro Tone to his master or order whenever cal'ld for, Also in case of any misfortune happening to or befalling sd Negro Tone previous to an answer respecting him, to pay his master or order whatsoever money shall be due him at sd time, and further in the case of death or desertion of sd Negro after an answer from Colo Greene intimating a desier to have him in his Regt., to pay Mr. Griffith the price allowed.

I hereby certify the above to be a true copy sent to Mr. Luke Griffith concerning his negro Tone.

Joseph Burchinal.

Source: Louise Lewis Lowell, *Israel Angell: Colonel of the 2nd Rhode Island Regiment* (New York: The Knickerbocker Press, 1921), 120.

In January 1778, Colonel Christopher Greene and other officers of the First Rhode Island Regiment returned home to raise a regiment of Black soldiers. In February, the state legislature passed a law that offered freedom to all slaves who were accepted into the regiment, with promises of reimbursement to their owners. Some 130 men were recruited into the unit, which served with distinction until the end of the war.

Richard Platt to Timothy Pickering

Dr Sir   Camp Valley Forge 31st of March 1778
        Your Note of the 26th. of January to me respecting Cash, lent by you, to Ensign Wales of Col^o Durkee's Reg^t., has been laying in my hands to no purpose, which I am very sorry for.—
        Ensign Wales is still out on Detachment & has been the whole winter—
        Genl McDougall has recovered of his Illness & has gone to Fish Kills, to take the Command there—I expect to follow him to morrow, & have requested the favor, of Adj^t. Marvin, belonging to the same Reg^t. with Ensign Wales, to get the Money of him, & leave it with Col^o. Scammell, which you may rely on, he will do, with a great deal of pleasure, as he has promis'd. I have put your Note into his Hands, that he (Ens. Wales) may not dispute it—
        There is no news in Camp—We are in hourly Expectations of having the Proceedings of the Committee, from Congress, with their Sanction—Conjectures here are various respecting them—I imagine some will be offended, others injured & many pleas'd therewith—I am Dr Col^o. with Esteem & Regard Your most Obed^t. Servant

Source: Timothy Pickering Papers, Massachusetts Historical Society.

Clement Biddle to Moore Furman

Dear Sir,   Moorhall April 1, 1778
        The Direction of the Forage Department & forming Magazines thereof being now solely under my Care I have to request the favour of you to undertake the purchase of five thousand bushels Grain preferring Oats Corn & Rye to Wheat and One hundred Twenty Tonns of Hay to be stored at or to near Pitts Town—you shall be

allowed such Commission as I shall fix & inform you of in a few Days & employ persons proper to receive & issue it—

I would have the hay all put up in bundles for which purpose I beg you will as soon as possible have one or more Screw presses erected for puting up the hay for the quantity now orderd & what may be got after the hay harvest—

You will naturally conclude that this request is extraordinary when I know how you have fared for the service, you have already done & been kept out of your Money—but I can assure you that Col°. Cox is now gone to York & will not return til he brings a sum sufficient to carry on our Department with Reputation & you may rely on having a proper supply for the business now requested & another to pay off old Forage Accounts—

I beg to have your Answer to the above also respecting the limits I should fix to the following purchasers to avoid interferring with each Other & whether Any but Pitts Town is Convenient to you—viz

	Grain	Tons hay
Sherrards	6.000	fixed
Col° West	10.000	d°
R Hoops Esq.	10.000	d°
Wm Lowry	5.000	d°
Pitts Town	5.000	M T
Coryells	2.000	
Hackets Town	6.000	none
Sussex Court h°.	6.000	none
Morris Pompton &c.—		

Your Answer thereto will much Oblige D^r. Sir Y^r. Mo: Obed. Servt.

Source: Record Group: Department of Defense; Subgroup: Revolutionary War; Mss. 4663, Division of Archives and Records Management, New Jersey State Archives. Furman was Deputy Quartermaster General at Pittstown, New Jersey.

Joseph Holt to George Washington

May it Please your Excellency   April 1st 1778
I beg your Approbation to my Resignation my reasons I hope will appear good to your Excellency

I have for several Months been in a low declining state of health which has put it out of my power to do my duty in the Reg^t. as an Officer, I frequently apply'd to Able Physicians but to no purpose, they have caution'd me strictly against Heats And Colds or fatigue as they Judge my Complaint proceeds from a Consumptive state, My disorder increases fact which Alarms me very much, I am truly sorry to quit the Army as it was my intention to Continue in the service while men were wanting, but as I am by Direction of Providence rendered incapible of serveing my Country any longer in the field I think it my duty to myself and Public to retire from the Army in hopes to find some remedy for the fatal disease that is fast growing on me I am y^r. Excellencys Most Devoted Most Obedient Hum^l Servt

NB The late death of my Father called me home to settle his Affairs, but Except the Above nothing Could prevail on me to leave the field

Source:, RG 93, M 859, Roll 110, Document 31344, National Archives.
Holt was a Lieutenant in the Fourth Virginia Regiment. His resignation was accepted the same day.

John Chaloner to Henry Champion

Sir   Commissarys Office Valley Forge Apl 2^d. 1778
          Yours of the 25th. Ulto. came to hand this Moment in the absence of Col: Blaine, in answer to which I have to say that the Colonel is confident of your exerting every nerve to serve the Genl cause—
          After thanking you for the supplies you have rendered the Army, & which whilst dispersed & in Winter Quarters have been sufficient for the support—
          I must add that it will be necessary to increase the Number of Cattle very speedily; As His Excellency purposes bringing the Army into the field very Early Recruits daily arrive & our numbers in the Course of a Month will be greatly augmented—His Excellency has desired me to write you to order the Drovers to cross Delaware at Easton, this Road will afford more Forrage, & so high up the Country as will prevent the fatigue of the Troops escorting them—I shall comply with your Request in shewing your Letter to the Genl. & forward it to Col Buchannan—Your scheme of securing the fish will be of essential

service & hope you will procure a large Quantity—we have adopted the same means to the Southward, I would Recommend Shad Fish only— I am Sir Your most Obed^t. hble Servt.

Source: Ms. 69492, Connecticut Historical Society.

Elias Boudinot to Horatio Gates

Dear Sir   Camp April 4th 1778
    Having sent Orders to Mr Peters for the immediate sending forward all the Officers detained at Hanover as well as those at York Town—I think it necessary to inform you, that General Lee is permitted to come to Camp and I have entered into the Exchange of Colonel Allen for Colonel Campbel.
    I hope you have received my last Letter of the [writer's blank] March. Am in Haste Dr Sir Your very Hble Servt

Source: RG 360, Papers of the Continental Congress, M 247, Roll 91, i78, v2, p451, National Archives.

John Francis Vachy to John Lamb

Sir   Camp Valley forge April 6th. 1778
    I take the Liberty to direct you these Lines to offer my Services in your Reg^t. t'is not By inconstancy Neither By dissatisfaction from any individual whatever that I am inclined to quit the Reg^t. Where I am, but only to find me in a Constant Place; moreover your person gives me reason to employ your protection— (and thereby the approbation of your officers) and if therefore I Can have the Hapiness to have it, Be persuaded Sir that my Behaviour Will give you no reason to be disgusted of Me.
    your answer will determine the Wish that I have to be to your orders, and i Will not go without his Excellency's leave.—I am with the most Respectfull Sentiments Sir Your most humble Servant

Source: John Lamb Papers, Manuscript Department, The New-York Historical Society. Vachy was Surgeon of the Fourth New York Regiment. Lamb was Colonel of the Second Artillery Regiment. See Henry Beekman Livingston to Robert R. Livingston, March 25 and 27, 1778.

Alexander Scammell to John Sullivan

Dear General,   Camp Valley Forge April 8th 1778.
Our Army is well recovered of the small Pox. Thank Heaven
& and General Howe's Supiness for permitting us to lay still under
innoculation. Clothing is coming is, so that I hope we shall be able to
clothe our brave, patient soldiers, (the most virtuous men living) in a
short time. Recruits begin to come in, & I am in hopes the foundation
laid for a plentiful supply of provisions & forage. The Baron Steuben
set us a truly noble example. He has undertaken the discipline of the
army, & shows himself to be a perfect master of it, not only in the
grand manoeuvres, but in every minutia. To see a gentleman dignified
with a Lt. Generals commission from the great Prussian Monarch,
condescend, with a grace peculiar to himself, to take under his
direction a squad of two or twelve men, in capacity of a drill Sergeant,
induces the officers & men to admire him, & and improve exceeding
fast under his instructions—I wish the enemy may be drove off from
Rhode Island time enough to admit of your joining the Grand Army to
lay Siege to Philadelphia. Now or never may be the proper motto of
America—and what cant she do, under the smiles of Providence, if
she collects what forces she may at Philadelphia & the other parts
held by the enemy, her supernumerary men are sufficient—our
Expectations are highly raised that you will clear the locusts off the
garden of New-England. Our Army & operations are much injured by
the delay of Congress in not fixing the new arrangement. A Pitt is
much wanted in our Senate. The wheels of Government drag heavily
like Pharaoh's chariot wheels. Indeed the different directions of
wheels within wheels must necessarily clash with each other, &
finally overset the load, unless more skillfully & spiritedly managed.
Hoping that this campaign will terminate the dispute, & that you may
be able after your long absence & extreme hardships, to retire with
laurels to your library, Mills, &c. &c. enjoy domestic ease. Your Most
Obd^t & Very H^{ble} Servt

Source: *The Historical Magazine* 2nd ser. vol. 8 (September 1870): 142-43.
Sullivan was a Major General from New Hampshire. He had been at Valley Forge until
mid-March and now had an independent command at Rhode Island.

James Mitchell Varnum to George Washington

Sir—   Camp April 8th. 1778
        Upon reviewing my Expences for the Winter past, I find
myself greatly in Arrear to my private Fortune. This is not the Result
of Extravagance in eating, drinking or Cloathing. There is no
conceivable Prospect of being in a better Situation. I am therefore
under the Necessity of establishing a Credit with a Person in Rhode
Island, upon whom, I can occasionally draw for Supplies. I know of
but one Way of affecting this, and that is by selling or mortgaging a
Real Estate, which I now own in that State. My Father in law has
supplied me, during the last Campaign, to the Amount of six Hundred
Dollars; But I cannot think of getting any more in that Way as he
supports my Family solely, without making me Debtor.
        The agreeable and important Obligations due to the Feelings of a
virtuous, fine Woman make me unhappy in being so long absent from
her, & I have too much Youth on my side to bury, in the Profundity of
Philosophy, the most pleasing Sensibilities of the human Heart.
        For these two Reasons I think it my Duty to apply for Liberty of
absence for the Term of five or six Weeks previous to the probable
Opening of the Campaign, and when other Circumstances will best
admit of it.—If the Division would be likely to suffer; I imagine General
Parsons might be called here in the interim to supply my Place; For I am
certain he is of no Service where he is.
        If your Excellency should judge this Request improper, I shall
chearfully acquiesce, and charge the Loss of domestic Felicity to the
good of the Service. For I do not think it delicate or consistent to repine
at Events which happen in a Sphere above my own proper Command.
        Your Excellency's Determination shall convince me what is
right in the matter, To know which will be gratefully felt by your very
obd^t. humble Servant.

Source: George Washington Papers, Roll 48, Library of Congress.
Despite his plea, Varnum was not able to leave for Rhode Island until mid-June.

Thomas Bradford to Elias Boudinot

Dear Sir   Camp Valley Forge April 11 1778
        I have with some difficulty this Day got off, (not being able to
do it before) Two loads of Flour, of 10 Blls each, for the City—On the

9th arrived, express, the brother of Mr Robt Haughy with the inclosed letters, which I send you to shew his wants & the inattention or willful neglect of Mr Ferguson or some others, in the City, to our letters, with a design, no doubt, to give us all the trouble they can—

I have not rec'd an answer to my letter of the 31st to Mr Ferguson a copy of which, with what I wrote him this Day, & my letters to Messrs Franklin & Haughey, I here inclose, hoping they will meet your approbation—I told Mr Haughey's brother that you would no doubt remit as soon as cash arrived from Lancaster—Please to write me what further you would choose to say to him & I will dispatch it by express—

I here inclose you sundry letters, two unopened suppose from Mrs Boudinot—This day arrived 11 or 12 prisoners from Trenton 6 or 7 of them seamen, I shall forward them tomorrow to Lancaster—Capt Fenwick is not yet come to hand from Reading—I should have dispatched the inclosed sooner, but have been so unwell ever since you left this that two Days of the time I have not been able to go abroad— Hoping you meet no great obstruction in your present business & that we shall soon see you in Camp I remain Dr Sir Yours &c.

Thos Bradford

Copy of a Letter from B to H Ferguson   March 31 1778
Sir

It being necessary to send a further supply of Flour for our Prisoners in Philad^a, this is to request that you would please to forward to me a Passport for two Shallop loads of Flour from below Willmington—The Shallops will be navigated by a Capt & two hands each—Your speedy Compliance will   Oblige yours &c

Copy of a Letter from TB to   H H F April 10 1778
Sir

We are still wanting an answer to a letter I wrote you by Mr Robt Haughey of the 12th ult & to mine of the same subject dated March 31, by which means flour for our prisoners of which I find they stand in need, has been & is still prevented being sent to them; I am now to request you would write me by the Bearer, who has it in charge to wait your orders—

Copy of a Letter from TB to Tho[s] Franklin   April 11 1778
Sir
    Herewith you will receive 20 Blls of Flour—You would long since have rec'd a large stock, as it has been purchased & lying ready to ship ever since Jan[y] last, had it not met with unnecessary delays—Verte

Source: Elias Boudinot Papers, Manuscript Division, Library of Congress. Boudinot was at a meeting with British representatives at New Town, Pennsylvania, to discuss prisoner exchange.

Thomas Craig to Thomas Wharton Jr.

Sir   Camp Valley Forge April 12th. 1778
    Though we were much distressed for want of Cloathing, when supplied from the Continental Store, We still rested satisfied, knowing that we always got a proportionable part, and that it was not in the Power of the States to procure a Sufficient for the Army,—But since each State has undertook to cloathe it's own Troops I have found, in taking a View of the Pennsylvania Line, that some Regiments are well cloathed, and in fact have more than they are present want while others, whom I will presume to say are as deserving as any, have not sufficient to cover their Nakedness.—
    This Sir, must certainly excite a Jealousy, and indeed I am sorry to say, that there must be partiality in it.—
    The present deplorable Situation of my Regiment, Obliges me to trouble you, therefore must beg you will order me down a small supply. I refer you to Cap[t]. Thomas Moore for the returns; They are moderate and only meant to cover the men we have doing Duty in Camp.—
    The two Officers who were sent to recruit for my Regiment are return'd with four recruits and say that it is not in their Power to get men. I have pointed out a Way to Cap[t]. Moore which he will communicate to you. I think it will be of Service & hope it may meet with your Approbation if not should be glad to have the speediest Steps taken you may think proper.—I have the Honor to be with much Esteem & respect Y[r]. Honor's Most Ob[t] hu[l]. Serv[t].

Source: RG 27, Roll 13, Frame 1149, Pennsylvania Historical and Museum Commission. Craig was Colonel of the Third Pennsylvania Regiment.

Henry Lee Jr. to Henry Laurens

Sir,   Valley forge Camp 15th. April 78.
The high value, which the Delegates of a free people have been pleased to affix to my services, is extremely flattering, and demands my most thankful acknowledgements.

To merit, by my future behavior, a continuation of the same favourable sentiments from your very respectable body, shall be the object of my unremitted zeal, and most strenuous endeavours.

While I pay this Just tribute of thanks to the directing power of America, permit me to tender to your Excellency, my very sincere respects for the obliging terms in which you have been pleased to notify me my appointment. I have the honor to be Sir with most perfect respect your most obed^t humble Servt.

Source: RG 360, Papers of the Continental Congress, M 247, Roll 96, i78, v14, p217, National Archives. Lee had been promoted to Major and given command of a "separate corps" by an act of Congress on April 7, 1778.

John Laurance to Timothy Pickering

Dear Sir,   Camp Valley Forge April 17th. 1778
I have been favoured with your obliging Letters of March 17th. and April 1st. which I thank you for. I should have answered them sooner, had the necessary attention to the Duty of my Department permitted—

I have fully considered the matter you mentioned; and am willing to make the Experiment of the Secretaryship if the Allowance is not less than 100 Dollars per month if you can obtain it for me—I can but try it, and if it will not maintain me I can look further a field—As it is a Duty every man in my Situation owes to his Family when an advantage is proferred him, to accept of it when it is not in compatible with the Service he owes his Country I make no doubt of being able of obtaining permission to resign my present Employment should you be able to get me appointed.

I sincerely thank you, for the Trouble you have taken respecting the matter Your interesting yourself in my favour gives me much pleasure as it shews a Friendship which I highly Value, and which I wish to preserve.

M^r. Boudinot is returned he is now surrounded with Paper and is so constantly employed; as not to have a leisure Moment to write to a Friend. He desires me to make his Compliments Acceptable—We quarter at the old Place. I am Your obliged humble ser^t.

Source: Timothy Pickering Papers, Massachusetts Historical Society.
Laurance was Judge Advocate General of the Continental Army.

William Bradford Jr. to Tacy Wallace

My dearest Tacy,   Camp April 21, 1778
        Where I disposed to forget as much as I am thinking of you, it would be out of my power to do so. I carry so many proofs of your kindness about me, that Ellerslie frequently obtrudes itself upon my mind even in my most busied hours—yet ever welcome will that idea be which reminds me of that sister in whose affection my heart finds so large a portion of its happiness.

        I heartily wish for an end of this cruel War which separates the dearest friends & banishes the social & domestic pleasures. But tho' I long for peace I hope our rulers will never purchase it upon base terms. Such terms it is said will be offered soon—for I call any terms base & dishonorable which imply a dependence upon G. Britain when we have bled & suffered so much in resisting her Tyranny. A very extraordinary speech delivered by Ld North is published in the Philada Papers. He says that the power of America is much Greater than any man would have imagined—that it will require length of time and much expence to subject us—& therefore he proposes that [com]missioners be sent over with *ample* powers to [neg]ociate a reconciliation—to disclaim the parila[men]tary right of Taxation—except such as are [neces]sary for the regulation of commerce—& [it] shall be disposed of by the state or provinci[al] word to put us in the situation we were in [before] 63 with some additional securities of our freedom. [He c]omplains of Genl Howe—says hat he himself has [done] everything that a good minister could do—has [furn]ished the General with Troops with money & [provi]sions in plenty—but that he could not command success without the endeavors of the Commander in Chief—That he is well assured Genl Washington has always been inferior to Howe in Numbers—This is the substance of the speech as related to me (for I have not seen it) and have no doubt it will produce very disagreeable consequences. It will give the disaffected among us an opportunity to raise a clamor & will gull others who long for peace on any Terms—Hostilities I hope will not cease while the Enemy continues in the Country—if we must negociate—let us negociate & fight at the same time—

Give my love to Mr Wallace—inform him that he will oblige me extremely by sending the boots pr first opportunity—Yet why request this—I know his kindness & attention—

I have not purchased the Tea—I expect Mrs Fisher will be out soon & that I will trust the management of the affair to her—With love to all I am My dear sister Your very affectionate

P. S. I brought away one of your Keys by mis[take] I left my own behind. Yours I have sent [   ] who no doubt will forward it to you.

Source: *Pennsylvania Magazine of History and Biography* (July 1916): 341-42.

Samuel Carlton to Timothy Pickering

Dear Sir,   Camp Valley Forge April 22[d]. 1778
I have long waited for a favourable opportunity to write to you. I am happy in having so an One as by M[r]. Millet. I Congratulate you with the pleasing News of the health of your Good Lady and your Noble Little Son with the Rest of your friends—
As to News here in Camp it would be impossible for me to give any Account to be depended on, there are so many Various Reports, One day a french War the next Contradicted, there is scarce a day but more or less Deserters Come out from the Enemy, But Differ so much in their recounts that there is not much to be Relied on from any of them—
This I have the pleasure to inform you, that it is a General Time of health in Camp, and lately the Soldiers tolerable Comfortable as to Cloathing &C—
must Beg the Favour of you to assist me in gitting into the Sea Department if any Vacancy, I would not wish to have any Officer Displaced for me—But if there should Be an Oppening would take it As a particular Favour Done me if I Can git into the Sea Service, as I imagin I Could be of more Service in that Department that in the land Service, That is if Can be of any Use any where—Must beg the

favour of you to Bear my Best Respects to the Honourable General Gates, & would Beg his Assistance with you—
For further particulars must Refer you to the Bearer,—For Hast Beg leave to Conclude—from y^r. Sincear friend & Humb Servt.
PS
S^r. should wish to have a line from you I have not heard from you Since ye 20th Feb would beg the favour of you (in Convenient to furnish us with such Resolves of the Honourable Congress as Relates to the Army

Source: Timothy Pickering Papers, Massachusetts Historical Society.

Baxter How to Sebastian Bauman

Honored Sir   April y^e. 23 1778
    I Rec^d. your Letter beareing date the 10th. Instant am Extremely glad to hear you are well or in a fair way to be So, altho you have been troubled with those Disagreeable things Call^d. Boyls—tis Said they are wholesome I wish you may find it So and that you may Come out of your Course of phisick as well fitted for a new Campain, as the fertile Ground which has long laid Covered in Snow Seems to be renew^d. by the breases of the South, and the warm Shining of the Sun
    Your Chest which I had Sent to Mr Kemper's to be brought to you, is Still there and agreeable to your Directions Shall be Detain^d.
    Genl. Knox is Indeed arived in Camp, but very Little is Said on any matters that were before in agitation, his presence Seems to Satisfy many that before accounted themselves agrieved, the Case is we want Sumbody that has Resolution we want a Bauman or Doughty; indeed you are much wanted in Camp you S^r. are not to be frightened by the presence of any man nighther will you be Charmed to Silence where Justice Call^d. you to Speak—Genl. Knox is Indeed very Complasent and is Got into the park to Live and with Great familiarity Takes a Game of Ball almost Every day—but I Dont learn as we are Like Ever to have the Corps Settled on that Respectable footing as I flattered my Self in a former Letter—However he promises that the arrangement of our Reg^t Shall Shortly be made out. we wait anxiously to See it, I presume it will afford m[   ] of Speculation, I hope you will be hear to anemadvert upon the Same—

Mr Kemper has informed me he has a Case of Instruments, and I have Contracted with him for the Same if you will be Kind anough as to Secure them for me and bring them with you to Camp, I shall Esteem it as a Singular favour

We have no material news in Camp, parties are Continually Coming to Camp and Last Evening a fine Reg^t: Arived from Virginia.

my duty to your Lady I present and Love to your Children whom I Respect for there father and Her Husband Sake I am with the Greatest Respect your most Hum^l. Servant

The Rest are all well and desire to be remembered to you—Jasper Stymetts has been very Sick he was Sent to the hospital, but he is much better now and I hope will be able to Join again

Source: Sebastian Bauman Papers, Manuscript Department, The New-York Historical Society. How was a First Lieutenant in the Second Artillery Regiment.

Robert Hanson Harrison to Timothy Pickering

Camp 23^d April 1778

My love to you my friend. What think you of the present complexion of Affairs?—Heaven grant, that Congress may fix the Army upon a good & satisfactory establishment. The one submitted by his Excellency to the Committee is the only one which can, in my opinion, retain the Officers. day after day and Hour after Hour, shew new causes of discontent and produce new resignations. Were we to continue fi[ ] persevering, all would be well.—The present, or, perhaps more properly, intended overtures of Britain, without great management will give us a severe shock. How it happens, but so it is that the great—the many unparalled injuries we have received—have not entirely done away old attachments in too many.—I wish the people, who are fond of peace and tired of War, may not be caught with the delusive bait now being hung out. Britain is certainly pushed. The proceed^g of Ministry must be founded, either in a despair of their own power to carry their points, or on some Europen rupture actually existing, or that will take place. I can not place any measure that has the least semblance of right to the credit of those men; nor can I consider their conduct in the light of finesse allegd them. Lord North has played too deep for that. By a Philadelphia paper, I find there is a Letter dated in London, tho probably manufactured in Philadelphia, or perhaps in Britain for the purpose, explaining the reasons of his conduct—Viz that it was to fall in with the claims of the Minority & to silence all further opposition by 'em. Be things as they may, It appears to me, that instead of remitting we should double our exertions. If we are still to war, we shall be the more able—If to treat, we can do it with more dignity and honor & more to our interest. It is confidently reported & I believe that fact is so, that Sr Wm Howe is recalled & Genl Clinton is to succeed him. An Exchange of Officers is agreed to this I tell you with pleasure, because I have felt concern for their many sufferings and because I'm no stranger to your sympathy. We are all well.

I am in great Haste, yet must request you to believe, that I retain a very affect^t attachment to you, and that I am Yr fr^d &

Source: Timothy Pickering Papers, Massachusetts Historical Society.

Clement Biddle to Moore Furman

Moorhall 25 April 1778

The Orders for forming Magazines of Forage in Jersey are founded on the principle of Collecting a quantity of the different Species on the river Delaware so high up as to be out of immediate Danger from the Enemy and that it may be drawn from thence by water to supply the Army on either side the river—the Quantity to be layd in and (constantly kept up as it is conscerned & drawn from thence) Coryells upwards on the Jersey Shore as high as it can be conveniently Collected and to Eight-Ten & fifteen Miles from the River is Forty Thousand Bushels of Grain prefering Oats Corn Rye, spelts Barley Buckwheat & the offal of wheat to whole Wheat & avoiding any interference with the Commissary of Provision's purchases as much as possible—Seven hundred Tonns of hay will be wanted at such places as can be most conveniently collected in that Country, to be put up in bundles for which purpose screw presses are to be erected at the most sutable places & persons employd to put up the same—A quantity of Straw to be collected at the Magazines on the river as a regular supply of that Article is the only substitute for Hay which cannot be got in the quantities requisite to keep the horses in Order.—indeed too much Straw cannot be got as the Consumption is very great—

The next general Object is to keep up a supply of Forage on the route from the North river to the Delaware—a magazine at Sussex Courthouse & Hackets Town—one at Pompton & another at the Clove with a supply at Morris Town keep up the Communication by the upper & lower roads.

At Trenton Princeton & Allen Town small Magazines of Hay & Grain to be constantly kept up, not more than three of four thousand Bushels of Grain & A proportion of hay on hand at one Time—these to be encreased as Occasion may require & Eight or Ten thousand bushels Grain & a proportion of hay & straw may be layd in for the purpose at the most safe & convenient places not in great Quantities at any One place—The situation & Quantities in this quarter Circumstances must determine—At present the Consumption there is Considerable from the Cavalry being quartered in that Vicinity—

Anexed is List of such places as I had thought of for Forage Magazines & the persons employ'd at them—I leave it to you to Employ or dismiss them & to make your Terms with them in the best manner you Can & you will employ from time to time such persons as are necessary for receiving issuing storing packing Hay, Cuting & Straw. Waggons, horses & other Carriage; all which must be subject to your Direction—anexed is also Copy of such Instructions as I have given for purchasing & for receiving & delivering Forage in this State—these will be some Guide to you but your Discretion must direct any necessary Alterations & Amendments in the State of New Jersey in which [the] Forage Department is to be subject to your Controul & Direction—M^r. Lawrence to be Continued (subject thereto) in purchasing for Princetown Trentown & Allen Town & I recommend him as a sutable person for the QM^r. Department—

M^r. Caldwell has purchased Quantities of Hay near Springfield Qm^r. Williamson under him at Elizabeth Town—large quantities may be got there & removed to Morris Town & on the route—M^r. Daniel Marsh at Raway was formerly employd by me—he was very useful & his Knowledge extensive & Industry great—I refer to his Letter enclosed—he has a screw press erected at Raway which could be employd & would enable us to remove the hay from thence—

I shall write to the persons who have Acted under me to apply to you for Employ, directions & money—the latter of which I will endeavour to keep you well supplied with—All accounts of Forage Carriage thereof & persons employ'd in that branch to be kept separate & settled for with me—

I shall give you such Information & Instructions from time to Time as the Service may require & request to hear from you as fully & often as possible—

You are to pay all Accounts for forage from the 2^d. day of March inclusive also for the keeping the light Cavalry at the Rates established by Law in New Jersey—the Vouchers for keeping the light horse should be signed by the Officer Com^g. the Regiment, by the Qu^{r}M^r. of by M^r. McCaskey Forage M^r of Cavalry—the latter was lately supplied with money for pay for the light horse but not sufficient—

For the old Accounts of Forage in Jersey if you will appoint a person to receive them (for which purpose to Attend different days at Different places) & give the Inhabitants a receipt for their Vouchers & Accounts on their being sent to me such as can be passed shall be transmitted to York Town & then Money drawn to discharge them which shall be sent (as soon as Obtaind) to Jersey with orders to discharge such as are allowd—this is the Only method in my power to being them to settlement—the money under the New Arrangement cannot be applied to them.

The County of Sussex remaining under Col^o Hooper your Direction of the Forage Department is not to Extend there so as to interfere with his purchases—

Source: RG Department of Defense, Subgroup Revolutionary War, Series: Numbered Manuscripts, Mss. 4664, Division of Archive and Records Management, New Jersey State Archives.

Anthony Wayne to William Irvine

Dear Colonel   Mount Joy 27th April 1778.

It's with the sincerest pleasure I Congratulate you on your Exchange—and hope to see you in Camp in the Course of a few days where you are much Wanted

The Intelligence out of Phil^a is, that the Hessians are Ordered home—but to this I can't give much Credit—as Mr. Howe could not possibly keep the City were they to be Withdrawn.

The Commissioners are said to be Lord Amhurst, Adm^l Kepple & Genl Murry, whose names sounds more like *Heralds of War*—than *Ambassadors of Peace.*
Adieu and believe me yours most Sincerely

Source: *Pennsylvania Magazine of History and Biography* 40 (1911): 109.
Irvine was Colonel of the Seventh Pennsylvania. He had been captured in June 1776, and had just returned in a prisoner exchange.

Ephraim Blaine to Charles Stewart

Dear Sir   Camp Valley Forge 2nd. May 1778
When you are at York Town many things may Offer in company with Members of Congress wherein you can be of great Service to me,—and it is Amendments I am Determined to have if I continue in my present Employ, 1st that the Deputy Commissary Genl. shall hold his Appointment as usual and have his Commission from Congress, shou'd he be so unfortunate as to be taken Prisoner that he might be treated as a Gentleman and Exchangable as such, 2^{nly}. the public to pay his Clerks and traveling Charges 3rd. because there is no Equivalent in the pay and Commissions allow'd by Congress to the Quarter Master Genl. the Comiss^y. Genl. the Forrage Master Genl. and their Deputies and assistants, the Deputy Q^r. M. Genl. have two PCent all Clerks and expencies paid the Assistant Deputies 1 ½ PCt. all charges paid, the Forrage Master the same, the Commissary Genl. half a P Cent upon the Whole Purchases, the Deputys half a P Cent upon their Districts, and the assistant purchasers 2 PCent, 4^{thly}. puting in a Commissary General who is was [*sic*] an entire Stranger two and giving him full Power to appoint suspend and Displace every person in the Department at pleasure without making any reserve for those who were in the employ and faithfull, my Character which I ever wish to support will I make no doubt did Induce Colonel Wadsworth to Offer me the preference which he has done, of the Middle District,— all men have their feelings upon this Ocasion though I do assure you I never had nor wanted to be higher in the Department than I was, but in that Station wou'd wish to be supported and hold every advantage with respect of my Commission I formerly did,—those Circumstances when I reflect & and am concious I have discharged my duty with Diligence & Integrity, and have ever since I have been in the public

Service made it my constant study to Keep down the unreasonable demands of the public Generally, and very Certain I have saved the public many thousands this I Assure you vexes me not a little, (but why should I reflect this was my Duty) you will please to pursue and make what Observations you think proper on this letter which wou'd wish to Mention to Congress in such a Maner as you think proper, wish you a Good Journey and am D^r. Sir Your Most Obed^t. Servt.

Source: Charles Stewart Collection, New York State Historical Association.
Blaine did not get everything he wanted, but continued as Deputy Commissary General of Purchases until December 1779, when he succeeded Wadsworth as Commissary General of Purchases.

Caleb North to Lord Stirling

May 2nd 1778

I Received your Note Yesterday Respecting the keeping a Guard Over the Tools: which we have at work at Redoubt N° 4: they were all Drawn by the Brigade Quarter Masters; to them the Officers Commanding the Fatigue Partys give their Receipts Every Morning and of Course Insist Upon Returning them in the Evening.—
I find it Impossible to Drive on this work for Want of Teams as they Never Come Out Until 10 Oclock—Notwithstanding I went to the Wagon master yesterday and Desired him to Be at the Redoubt by 8 OClock it is now Near Eleven and no Wagons Come as yetI am Sir y^{rs} &c &c

Source: Mrs. Archibald Crossley Autograph Collection, Library of Congress.
North was Lieutenant Colonel of the Eleventh Pennsylvania Regiment. The shortage of wagons and teams was a continuing problem.

Clement Biddle to Moore Furman

Dear Sir   Moorhall 5 May 1778
    I have your favour of 30 Ult^o.—The enclosed List contains all the persons immediately employ'd by me [no list found] & I have allow'd those who acted as Forage Masters 40 D^s. p month & 3 rations—such as purchased also I allow'd them Expences or about a dollar a day in addition to the other—M^r. Lawrence has a

Commission for purchasing which I have not settled & was to employ of the necessary persons under him—I wish you to extend your purchases to as great An Amount as possible—we should have in view not only supplying the Troops that come from the Eastward but the possible removal of our whole Army if the Enemy should shift their Opperations to the North river—tis our business & we are orderd to be prepared for all such Events—

The Iron which belongd to you I was informed of by Mr Loughead & Mr Barnhill—I took the Waggons down by Genl Orders—they kept the Account of the Number in each parcel (as there was more than yours) & directed them to be kept separate at J Sheas—One of them must have the Account.—My Clerk who gave an Order for some small parcels for immediate Use of the Army is Absent or I would send you an Account—it was but for small Quantities—I think Sheas has some Account of the Iron that might be useful to you in your procuring payment—I desire to have the returns as you mention & also an Account in the Interim of the quantities at each place I am Dr Sir Y^r mos. Obdt st

Source: Record Group: Department of Defense; Subgroup: Revolutionary War; Mss. 4667, Division of Archives and Records Management, New Jersey State Archives.

Charles Pettit to Moore Furman

Dear Sir   Moore Hall 5 May 1778
        Your two Favours of the 2^d., one directed to Genl. Greene and the other to myself are received—they came Yesterday Afternoon while we were both in Camp, but Mr Shaw Shews me a Receipt from the Waggon M Genl. for the two Teams.
        I was in hopes you would send us some good Team Drivers, at least that you would Man your own Teams; as Drivers being used to the same Team, or even coming from the same Part of the Country will understand the Horses, & they him better than a perfect Stranger, or one from a distance where the Manner of driving & breaking Horses may be widely different. And besides we really want some good Drivers & therefore wish you would make a Point of furnishing as many Drivers as Teams at least. If you can meet with any good Saddle Horses you will oblige Genl. Greene & myself by sending at

least one for each, such as you suppose we ought to ride; and as you have Taste in Horses I need not be more particular.

I have spoke to Col. Hooper about his People interfering in your District—he tells me that before your Appointment he looked upon the whole State as open to Purchases, but he will take Care there shall be no farther Interference.

The News from France I believe to be undoubtedly true, & we look for Official Information of it from Congress every Hour—when that arrives it will be announced by the Mouths of our Cannon—I am D Sir your Friend & hum^e Servt

Source: Record Group: New Jersey Department of State, Sub-Group: Military Records, Division of Archives and Records Management, New Jersey State Archives. Pettit was an Assistant Quartermaster General.
The "News from France" was on the signing of Treaties of Alliance and Commerce between France and the United States on February 6. The news was confirmed and a major celebration was held at Valley Forge on May 6.

Lewis Farmer, Daniel Burchart, George Nagel, Christian Febiger, and Peter Muhlenberg to the Continental Congress, Endorsed by Baron de Kalb

Camp at the Valley Forge the 6th. of May A.D. 1778
To the Honorable Congress of the united
American Independent States:
May it please Your Honors:
We the Subscribers humbly entreat wether it may please Your Honors to take the Materials of this our Petition into Your munificent Consideration. Your Honors have thought useful and necessary for the Cultivation of Mind, and Instigation as well as Propagation of Virtue to appoint and constitute Chaplains to every Brigade: We rejoice over Your paternal Care, in respect of such wholesome Regulation. But at the same Time beg Leave to represent to Your Honors that we lack one thing for to complete the good One and praise worthy Purpose of so salutary an In[tinsh]ion, and which incommodious for many, has been with held from Your Honors Consideration.

As there are divers religious Persuasions among Officers and Solders, who rejoice about the Privilege of religious Liberty as one important Object of our present Contest; so are no less Officers and Soldiers of different Languages a Seed which promiseth to us a flourishing Condition of our united States. There are many Germans also, Officers of every Rank, and no small Number of Soldiers under their respective Commands, the most Part thereof do not understand the principal Expressions of the English Tongue, and yet are obliged for mere form's sake to attend divine Service. How inconsistent this seems with Sound Reason, we find not necessary to explain to Your illustrious Minds. Besides this we perceive a very disagreeable Effect arrisng for it. The sensible Officer, unacquainted with the extensive Knowledge of the English Language very often expresseth his desire for an Amendment in regard of this. The German Soldiers do often grumble about their being neglected in offering the Means for Salvation, and being commanded to parade and attend divine Service in a Language unintelligible to them, they shew great Inattention, besides the base Ideas they fix against divine Service, which they are forced to frequent without the least Benefit for their Souls. Never the less, we can assure the Honourable Congress, that not only we, but our Soldiers also bear a due Regard for divine Service in our nativ Language, and by Consequence the good Effect will not fail to inlighten the Minds of many, to encourage them to virtuous Actions and prove to become the Soul of the military Vigour in many of them.

For these Reasons we the Petitioners humbly request, that Your Honors may be pleased to appoint and constitute one Chaplain to the Germans in our Army in general, who can in Connection with the German Regiment under Command of General Muhlenberg, preach to us, either by Turns, or if convenient for them altogether at one Instance of Time, that we may have the wishful Oportunity to unite in proper Attention to be edified in the Principles of Religion, and Prayers and Praises to God Almighty the Fountain of All Perfections and real Happiness for our independent States.

We beg further Leave to recommend to Your Honors Benevolence the Gentlemen who dispatches this our Petition, the Rev^d M^r. Henry Miller, whom we think fit for the Purpose, because many of us are acquainted with his unstained Character and Ability. We had the Pleasure to hear his divine Discurses at different Times in our German Language, whereby we were edified and our assembled Soldiers attentive and much pleased. He is the Gentleman, who has gained Your Favour formerly, being constituted Chaplain to Colonel Stewarts Regiment, where he preached English, which Dialect is not so fluent to him, as his nativ Language the German. All this we resign to Your Honor's Wisdom and Munificence, by which You have hitherto under divine Providence and Protection our present glorious Affairs conducted. A condescending Compliance with our humble Request will infinitely oblige Your Honor's most humble and dutiful servants

> Lewis Farmer Lt: Col: 13th P: R:
> Daniel Burchart Maj[r]
> Geo: Nagel Col 10th. P R
> Christian Febiger Colo 3 V. R.
> P: Muhlenberg B.G

at Camp near Valley forge May 6th, 1778. As I think it usefull and necessary for the German soldiers and others of the Same People that understand but their own Language. I think it incumbent on me as their Countryman, to join the Subscribers in their humble Petition to the Most Honourable the Congress. In granting the Request, I dare Say, these Soldiers will be better instructed in their Duty as Citizens, and an increase of Blessings to this Country will derive from their joined Prayers.

I also would recommend to the favour of the Supreme Council of the United States, the Rev[d] Henry Miller as a proper Person to be appointed to edify by examples of Morals as well as of Piety.

The Baron de Kalb

Source: RG 360, Papers of the Continental Congress, M 247, Roll 55, item 42, vol. 5, pp. 69-71, National Archives.
Congress promptly acted on the petition and appointed Miller as Brigade Chaplain on May 18, 1778. Farmer was Lieutenant Colonel of the Thirteenth Pennsylvania, Daniel Burchart was Major of the German Regiment, Nagel was Colonel of the Tenth Pennsylvania and Febiger was Colonel of the Eleventh Virginia. Peter Muhlenberg was a Brigadier General from Virginia and Baron de Kalb was a Major General from France.

Ephraim Blaine to Thomas Johnson

Honoured Sir—   Commissaries Office Camp May 7 1778
I have the pleasure of informing You that there is a good appearance of our being able to support the army with provisions. no difficulty in any article but meat, and hope if oeconomy be introduced in the army we shall be able to bear them along with that article also: I have a good prospect of laying up large quantities of imported salt, which will enable me to take the advantage of the Season in securing

pork; which must be the staple article in the meat Kind to feed the army with, therefore every encouragement ought to be given the Farmers to raise and feed large Quantities.—

A new Commissary General is appointed and sundry alterations made in his department respecting the purchase of Provisions. I have the honour of being appointed his Deputy for part of the State of New York, Jersey, Pennsylvania, the Lower Counties and Maryland. I mean to allott districts from each assistant purchaser, out of which they are not to buy any article, would request Your Honour and Council to recommend such persons as are suitable to transact that business they must be such as will give their whole attention to the publick good. Their districts must be large so as to afford them employ sufficient and make it worth their acceptance, their pay is two pr Cent upon all disbursements no allowance of Expences or Clerks. All charges upon the removal of Stores or driving and pasturing of Cattle to be paid by the publick, also Drovers wages and such charges as attend the forwarding of Live Stock and other provision to the army. Men who are too much confined to Domestick Life or have large engagements in either publick or private business will not answer. I could wish to have true and active whigs engaged. I have some men since last Year who are still employed and have been very faithfull those I mean to Continue and appoint them such districts are they are capable to Manage, amongst whom is Mr Richardson of Georgetown Mr Ford of St Marys, Mr Buchanan of Baltimore and one or two others.

The army will shortly be in want of all the Salt provision purchased and Stored to the Southward. The difficulty of removeing which has hitherto been found very great and attended with much delay. I shall be particularly obliged to You for your aid in ordering all the Salt provision purchased in Your State, either by Craft or Waggons to the Head of Cheseypaek or Charlestown

I shall esteem it as a particular favour to be honoured with a line from You and remain with due respect Your Honours Most Obedient hble Servt.

Source: Maryland State Papers (Red Books), MSA S989, MdHR 4587-11 Maryland State Archives.
Johnson was Governor of Maryland. As new recruits arrived, and veterans returned from furloughs, food shortages again plagued the Continental Army.

Charles Stewart to Samuel Gray

Sir   Commissarys Office Camp, May 10. 1778.
In expectation of receiving your returns, as well as M^r. Winships I put off waiting on Congress Until the 2^d. Ins^t: The pressing Calls for money to discharge the expence of my Department prevented my waiting Any longer; and as I did not know, what the Monthly expence of the Eastern Departm^{ts}. or Northern Army would amount to I was at a loss what sum to apply for to pay off the demands, & therefore requir'd of them only a present Supply, of which am ready to send you apart. The late Commissary General (M^r. Buchanon) has demanded the return of all Provisions & Stores received of him or his deputies up to the 15 Ins^t. soon after which he proposes settling his Acc^{ts}. & my attendance will Also be Necessary at Congress at that Time: I therefore beg you will have the returns & Acco^{ts}. of your District ready as soon as possible; those that are now ready, you will take care to send by the person you send for money.—if you don't come yourself. I am your Most obedient, Humble Servt.

Source: Samuel Gray Papers, Connecticut Historical Society.
Gray was Deputy Commissary General of Issues at Peekskill, New York.

Henry Knox to John Lamb

Dear Sir,   Camp, Valley Forge, 11th May 1778
I received your Favour pr L^t. Col^o. Oswald,—This will be delivered you by General Greene, who will make the proper Arrangements with you of the necessary Business in the Quarter-Master's Line, to transport to Head-Quarters, the Artillery and Stores which are at Farmington, all of which, except the two eight Inch Howitzers are to come on to Head Quarters. The two Howitzers will be better employed perhaps on the North-River. Besides the Artillery at Farmington, which consists of 15-6 Pounders—2-8 Inch Howitzers, and 10-4 Pounders,—and Nineteen Ammunition Waggons, and eight Tumbrils with stores.
The three brass twelve pounders now at and near Fishkill, and the one at Albany,—the brass twenty four pounder at New Windsor, and the two 24 Pounders at Albany, taken from General Burgoyne, are to

come on to Head-Quarters. You will take the proper Steps to have the 12 Pounder & the two 24 P^{rs}. brought from Albany as soon as possible.

As it is your Desire, you are to take the Command of all the Artillery mentioned and march them to Head-Quarters by such Route as General Greene shall point out to you. Major Stephens will command the Artillery on the River. You will settle with General Gates what Companies of yours shall be left at Fishkill. I think, after you have sent a Company to relieve Capt. L^t. Savage at Fort Schuyler, which you are to do according to your Proposal, you may order three or four of your strongest Companies on to this Camp. The others with Major Stephens's and such Draughts as General Gates shall please to annex to them, will, I should suppose, be sufficient for that Department. However, you will fix this Matter with General Gates.—

The Artillery at Farmington is compleated with Harness, port-Fires, Tubes, Ammunition &c. from Springfield, and ready to move as soon as the Horses shall be procured for that Purpose.—

General Greene will send a Quarter-Master to New-England, to procure the Horses for the Artillery, Waggons and Tumbrils, at Farmington, to transport which, it will require 210 Horses.—

You will fix with General Gates, the number of guards necessary for their Security from Farmington to Fishkill,—and His Excellency General Washington, will do the same with General Gates, from Fishkill to Head-Quarters.—

There are no Commissions at Head-Quarters, therefore cannot send the Commissions you request. I am Dear Sir Your Most Obedient Humble Servant

Source: John Lamb Papers, Manuscript Department, The New-York Historical Society. Washington was gathering his artillery for a possible siege of the British in Philadelphia.

Anthony Wayne to Henry Laurens

Sir   Mount Joy May 13th 1778
I am Informed that by a late Resolve of the Honorable Congress, one Clergyman only is to be allowed to a Brigade—this being the case I would wish to have a Chaplain Appointed to the first Penns^a. Brigade in whom I find the Gentleman, the Christian, and the Scholar—I mean Doct^r Robert Blackwell, (an Episcopal Clergyman) who has proved

himself a friend to his Country and is the Only Chaplain belonging to that Brigade.

I also wish to Recommend Doc.[r] David Jones as Chaplain to the Second Pennsy[a] Brigade—but as he has already been mentioned to Congress for that Office—I shall only say that he Merits every Indulgence from his piety care & Attention to the Line of his Duty—

I therefore wish to see two such Worthy Gentlemen Appointed as Chaplains to the Division which I have the Honor to Command—will you be so Obliging as to lay the matter before the Honorable Congress—and should it meet their Approbation—you will add to the Obligation by transmitting their Appointments the first Oppertunnity.

Interim I am with every Sentiment of Esteem your most Ob[t]. & very Hum[l]. Serv[t].

Source: RG 360, Papers of the Continental Congress, M 247, Roll 179, vol. 1, item 161, pp. 215-16, National Archives.
Congress appointed Blackwell as a Brigade Chaplain on May 21, and Jones on May 25, 1778.

William Bradford Jr. to Rachel Boudinot

My dear Rachel   May 14th 1778.

I find by a Letter from my father that you are on a visit at Trenton. I should be happy could you extend your Jaunt as far as full View—The Camp could now afford you some entertainment. The manoeuvering of the Army is in itself a sight that would Charm you.—Besides these, the Theatre is opened—Last Monday Cato was performed before a very numerous & splendid audience. His Excellency & Lady, Lord Stirling, the Countess & Lady Kitty, & M[r] Green were part of the Assembly, The scenery was in Taste—& the performance admirable—Col. George did his part to admiration—he made an excellent *die* (as they say)—Pray heaven, he don't *die* in earnest—for yesterday he was siezed with the pleurisy & lies extremely ill—If the Enemy does not retire from Philad[a] soon, our Theatrical amusements will continue—The fair Penitent with the Padlock will soon be acted. The "recruiting officer" is also on foot.

I hope however we shall be disappointed in all these by the more agreeable Entertainment of taking possession of Philad[a]—There are strong rumors that the English are meditating a retreat—Heaven send it—for I fear we shall not be able to force them to go these two months—

I scrawl these few lines to accompany a letter which I send to my Father—Love to sister Betty & all Friends. Adieu ma chere soeur, je suis votre.

Source: *Pennsylvania Magazine of History and Biography* 40 (1916): 342-43.
Rachel was Bradford's sister in New Jersey. Joseph Addison's play *Cato* was very popular with the Americans.

George Fleming to Sebastian Bauman

Dear Sir,   Camp, 14th May, 1778
My last to you was in answer to your Favor pr Corp[l]. Norestrant. The same Reason has prevented my writing to you since then, that, I make no doubt, prevented your writing to me—your expecting weekly to be here.

This I write at a venture, as I am doubtful whether you have set out for Camp or not.

Nothing is done yet, with regard to settling the Artillery Officers Rank—All lies dormant with fair Promises; which we have as usual. Gen[l] Knox told me that very shortly (but that was when he came from Boston, immediately on his arrival,) the Rank would be settled, and if in his power, to the satisfaction of the Old standing Artillery Officers. I told him that I should never submit, to be superceded by Cap[t]. L[t]. Archibald, which of course would be the Case, provided his Marching Regim[t]. Commission, is older than mine in the Artill[y], and the new Fangled preposterous Arraingement, which the new appointed Artill[y]. Officers are for, should take place. There is not an Officer of the Artillery Line that will continue if the new plan should be adopted.

Mons[r]. Duplisis is here, he enquired very cordially after you— and declared before two or three Generals, that you are the best American Artillery Officer in the Corps—that you thoroughly understood your business.—

L[t]. Col[l]. Fluere desires particularly to be remembered to you; Indeed all your Acquaintance here desire the same.

Recruits arrive in Camp very fast.—Our Men are in good health & high spirits. Joy sparkles in the Eyes of our whole Army.—

Great is the Change in this State since the News from France—the Tories All turned Whigs. They begin, mercenary Wretches, to be as eager for Continental Money now as they were a few weeks ago for Gold.—

No Doubt M^r. How has informed you of his being appointed Brigade Q^r. Master, and that Capt. Lieut. Reed has the Command of the Company.

M^r. Nestil continues just as you left him—over head & ears in Love!

You will much Oblige me by forwarding the inclosed.—

L^t. Col^l. Oswald is here, & says he expects Col^l. Lamb with four Companies of Artillery.

The new Regulations are not rec^d. in Camp yet, so that I remain Pro. Tem. still I—e—Capt Lieut.—By a Phil^a. News Paper we find England has declared War against France.—

I hope M^{rs}. Bauman & Family are well—With most respectful Compliments to them, I remain, Dear Sir, most unfeignedly, Your most Obe^d Servt.

P.S. About 50 Indians are just arrived in Camp from the Northard—a large Number are following them.—

Source: Sebastian Bauman Papers, Manuscript Department: The New-York Historical Society. The Indians were friendly Oneidas and Tuscaroras who came down from New York to act as scouts.

Charles Pettit to Thomas Wharton Jr.

Sir,   Camp Valley Forge. 16 May 1778.

Your Excellency's Letter of the 7th Instant came to my Hands in the Absence of General Greene, who is on a Tour to Fishkill. I am not insensible of the Justice of the Complaint you mention respecting the payment of Waggon-hire. The Applications I daily receive have fully convinced me that this Complaint is not only too well founded, but that it might be extended, with equal Justice, to many other Particulars, We have therefore, with Unabated Attention, endeavoured to remedy this Mischief, as well for the sale of the People who are the immediate Sufferers, as with View to facilitate the Publick Service; and I have the Satisfaction to inform you that our Endeavours have been so far successful, that I have good Reason to believe the like

Complaints will not arise in future. It was some Time after we came into the Department that we obtained our first Supply of Cash; we were therefore obliged, for a Time, to encounter the Difficulties that opposed us, with the Shattered Remains of Credit. But we are now possessed of more ample Funds: sufficient we hope to pay all our Current Contracts and to clear off the incumberances which has arise since Our Commencement, which was the 2nd. of March last. Many Debts I know are due on former Contracts, as we have Warmly Solicited Congress to have them discharged; but as we are not authorized to Intermeddle with them, I can not at present say when or how they will be settled. You may be assured however that nothing on Our Part Shall be Wanting, to render the Publick service as little inconvenient as possible to the Inhabitants of the Country.

The necessary Transportation of Stores and Forage is so great that we wish to improve the Little water Carriage left in our Power to the best Advantage. For this End we have got a number of Boats now in Use on Schuylkill, which answer the Purpose very well when the River is pretty full; but it is now so low that the Navigation, at many passes, is much obstructed, Major Eyre has Surveyed the River from Reading hither, and informs he that it may without Difficulty be rendered navigable through the summer Season for the Boats lately constructed which are calculated to draw but little Water in Proportion to the Burden they carry. This necessary Work though it would be beneficial to the United States for a Short, perhaps a very short Time only, would produce lasting Avantagse to the Commerce of this State; I am therefore induced to hope the Government will improve so favourable an opportunity of serving the common Cause and at the same Time so essentially promoting the Interests of the State. I am farther induced to make this Application to you from the Impracticability of engaging a sufficient Number of Hands through any other Channel to effect the Business with the necessary Expedition. The River is now low, and if a number of the People of the Country bordering on the River could be assembled at each of the passes nearest to their respective Habitations, the work might be completed in a very few Days. Major Eyre who was with me yesterday, will Wait on you in a Day or two, and will explain the Matter to you more fully. As it will be of great Importance to the Publick to have this Business speedily effected, I must beg your early Attention to it, whether the Expence is eventually to be borne by this State in particular, or by the United States; as in either case the Aid of the civil Government will be necessary. Major Eyre informs me the Evidence will not probably exceed two thousand Pounds. The inclosed Paper contains a Copy of his return of the Depth of Water and Remarks on the Different Passes that want Improvement. I have the Honour to be, with great Respect Your Excellency' most obedient & very humble Servant

Source: RG 27, Roll 14, frames 21-22, Pennsylvania Historical and Museum Commission. Complaints from civilians about the lack of payment for wagon hire, food, clothing, and support services were common, and were exacerbated by the declining value of the Continental currency. The proposed work to improve the passage of the Schuylkill River for the Army's supply boats never got underway.

Anthony Wayne to Henry Laurens

Sir   Camp at Mount Joy 16th. May 1778
        The Brigade late Conways—Composed of four Penns^a. Regiments in Major General Lord Stirlings Division—having no Chaplain—I would beg leave to Recommend Doct^r. McMurdy, belonging to the Eleventh Penns^a. Regiment as a Person well Qualified to Supply that Vacancy—he has been in the Service Since the Commencement of the War—& has Supported the Character of a Gentleman & a Scholar—I am with every Sentiment of Esteem
        Your Most Ob^t. and very Hum^l Ser^t

Source: RG 360, Papers of the Continental Congress, M 247, Roll 179, i161, p. 211, National Archives. Robert McMordie/McMurdie was not appointed Chaplain of the First Pennsylvania Brigade until July 15, 1780.

John Chaloner to Jeremiah Wadsworth

Sir   Commissaries Office May 17 1778
Colonel Blaine being absent, I take the Liberty of inclosing you Copy of a Letter I this day rec^d. from his Excellency. The Contents will doubtless point out to you the necessity and propriety of ordering immediately to Jersey a Quantity of Provision sufficient to feed thirty Thousand Men daily. I have taken the necessary steps for forwarding the flour, but must depend on your Deputies for the Eastern Department for Meat, which if provided I flatter myself the Troops

will not be retarded on their March by the Commissarys Department which I know will afford you singular Satisfaction. But on the other hand, a disappointment will to his Excellency be exceedingly mortifying, as also to yourself, to avoid which, be assured, of my utmost endeavours, and in the mean time I remain with due respect Sir Your most Obed^t. Servt.

Source: RG 360, Papers of the Continental Congress, M 247, Roll 104, i78, v33, p. 515, National Archives.

Charles Pettit to John Davis

Sir   Camp Valley Forge 17 May 1778
        As it is expected this Army may have Occasion to move from this Ground in a few Days, it becomes necessary to Collect in Camp our whole Strength of Teams as speedily as possible. You will therefore please to forward with all convenient Expedition all such Teams as you have or can quickly equip for the Service. Any Tents, Knapsacks or other Equipage which may be ready in your District you will please to forward with the Teams. Spare Harness is also much wanted. If the Commissary Genl. of Military Stores should want to forward anything to Camp your Teams can assist him. Such Teams as are not wanted for those Purposes you will order to load at the proper Places with Provisions or Forage, both of which are wanted. Some spare Horses will also be wanted, and as I am informed there are some Ammunition Waggons at Reams Town which the Quarter Master of Lancaster may not be able immediately to furnish with Horses, you will therefore please to send immediate Notice to him or to the Person acting at Reams Town what Number of spare Horses (I mean those you cannot equip in Teams) you expect to forward, that he may send back a Request to you for such as may be wanted for these Waggons—You will let this be done in Time for his Request to meet your Horses at Susquehanna. As we know not what Hour the Army may have Occasion to move, you will give the Business all possible Dispatch.
        M^r. Johnston Smith has probably collected a good Number of Teams. I know not where to direct to him and am much thronged with Business: I would therefore wish you to dispatch a Copy of this Letter, or such Parts of it as may be proper, to him, and desire him to follow the Directions it contains, as possibly some of the Teams may arrive in

Time to be useful on this Emergency. There is Reason to believe the Enemy are about to evacuate Philadelphia and the most probable Conjecture is that our Army will move towards New York. I am Sir, Your most humble Servant

Source: MG 275, Records of Pennsylvania Revolutionary War Era, 1771-1791 (Misc. Mss.), Pennsylvania Historical and Museum Commission.
Davis was Deputy Quartermaster General at Carlisle, Pennsylvania.

Clement Biddle to Moore Furman

Dear Sir,   Moor Hall May 18. 1778
I wrote you twice yesterday & sent 12000 Dollars by Mr Banker which I hope you received with the Letters as not A moment should be lost in laying in the Forage not knowing how soon we may want it, therefore I am sure you will exert yourself—
        The route from Howells ferry will require 2 to 3 or 4000 bushels at the Mill near there—as much or More (with proportion of hay & Straw at each) at Pitts Town & at any place in your District between there & Hackets Town two or three thousand bushels—from thence through Sussex Cot^y. West under Col^o. Hooper will lay in the necessary Quantities—
        The lower route you will please to pay the earliest Attention to as desired in my Letters—I am Dr Sir Your mo: Obed^t Ser

Source: RG: Department of Defense, Subgroup: Revolutionary War, Mss. 4654, Division of Archives and Records Management, New Jersey State Archives.
As more and more intelligence came in to indicate that the British intended to march through New Jersey, efforts began to establish magazines of food and forage in that state, in order to support the Continental Army as it pursued the enemy.

Richard Kidder Meade to Daniel Morgan

Sir   Head-Quarters, May 18, 1778
I am commanded by his excellency to desire that you will now keep the most vigilant watch over the motions of the Enemy, both Foot and Horse. It is particularly requisite at this time as a considerable detachment marched this day towards the lines on the other side of the

River which may perhaps induce the enemy to make a move out on this side. I am Sr Your mo obet s^t

P.S.—you will please to consult with Col^o Jackson at the Gulf that your parties may not fall in with each other—

Source: Theodorus Bailey Meyers Collection, No. 936, Manuscripts And Archives Division, New York Public Library.
Morgan was Colonel of the Eleventh Virginia and in command of an American outpost at Radnor, Pennsylvania. The detachment was the "Barren Hill Expedition under the Marquis de Lafayette.

Charles Pettit to Thomas Bradford

Dear Sir,   Moore Hall, 19 May 1778.
        General Lee has signified his Expectation of being in camp to morrow, and His Excellency has desired me to provide Quarters for him on the Right of the Army. I have sent an Officer round and can find no tolerable Prospect of accommodating him unless you and your Brother will be kind enough to remove from the Quarters you are in; in such Case other good Quarters shall be assigned you. Col. Biddle mentions to me Mr. Moses Coates's about a mile from hence, just back of his Quarters, where there is a good House and agreeable Family with every convenient Accommodation, and will probably suit you both at least equally well with your present Situation. The Necessity of providing Quarters in that Neighbourhood for Genl Lee obliges me to make this Request, and as it will so much tend to accommodate the Army and oblige Genl Greene and myself, I cannot doubt the ready Compliance both of your Brother (to whom my Compliments) and yourself. I am Sir Your most obed^t. hum^e Servt.

Source: *The Lee Papers, Vol. 2, 1776-1778, Collections of the New York Historical Society For the Year 1872* (New York: The Society, 1873), 393-94. Major General Charles Lee from Virginia, had recently been exchanged, having been taken prisoner in 1776.

Alexander Scammell to Allen McLane

Dear Capt Camp Valley Forge May 20th 78
I am happy that you with your brave little party have conducted with so much honor to yourself—Am sorry Lt Story has come under

Censure as I ever esteemed him a good Officer—The Marquis effected a glorious Retreat as well as a difficult one—One of the men sent me under Guard pretends that he was a deserter—wish you would inform me—I am suffering for want of a good Leather Ink pot, and a good Penn-Knife—If you have an Opportunity wish you would send into Philadelphia and procure those Articles for me—A double Ink pot admitting a pen on each side would best suite me, as it is most handy to carry in my Pocket. Y^r Very Humble Servt

Source: Allen McLane Papers, Manuscript Department, The New-York Historical Society.

Clement Biddle to Thomas Wharton Jr.

Sir   Moorhall 21 May 1778
        John Hemberger Powder Maker on French Creek called on me to inform me there was about a Tonn of Powder belonging to this State which would be completed in two Days—if you will inform me where you would choose to have it sent I will order a Waggon with it and a proper Guard—
        With Compliments to M^{rs}. Wharton & Miss Fishbowin I am sir with respect Your mo: Obed Servt

Source: RG 27, Roll 14, frame 78, Pennsylvania Historical and Museum Commisson.

Anthony Wayne to Sharp Delaney

                                              Mount Joy 21st May 1778
        Dear Sir,—Various are the reports and many the conjectures about the enemies quitting Phil^a. and the place they are Destined for—some say New York, others Halifax—but the more prevailing opinion is the West India Islands—for my own part I am not quite so sanguine as some others, about their avacuating their present post, without first offering us battle,—we were so fully Confident of their being about to embark last *Monday*—that a Detachment of upward of two thousand men under the Marquis *De Lafayette*, was sent down towards their lines to be Ready to take possession of the City as soon as they should

quit it—but the *Caitifs* made a forced march the night before last and threw themselves into his rear—and were on the point of surrounding him (at seven Oclock in the Morning) before he had the least Intelligence of their movement—however he made a happy escape by passing the Schuylkil at Matsons ford & possessing the *Gulf hills*— the Enemies van made its appearance on the one side as the Marquis's Rear arrived on the other—their numbers by every acct. was about 7000 who had actually thrown themselves in between the Marquis and our Camp—but by moving down towards Phila and Crossing at Matsons—he avoided (otherwise) Inevitable Distruction—the Enemy must have effected a march of upwards of twenty miles with that large body totally undiscovered thro' the Inattention of the Patrols.

they Returned to Phila last evening without either killing or taking a single man of ours. Several Deserters from the Enemy have come in with some Prisoners taken by our Light Troops and *Indians* hanging on their Rear—the latter at one fire killed five of the Enemie's Horse, and by the war Hollow put the Remainder to flight.

I have always hinted that its my opinion *Mr. Clinton*, will offer us battle—i.e. that after shiping all his stores & heavy artillery he will make a forward move in force, but he will never attack us on this Ground—he will either Retire after a Little Parade, Otherwise by taking post in our Rear near *Moore Hall* Manoeuvre us off the Ground.

this is all Conjecture—he may possibly leave this State without this parade—but that some Capital movement will take place in the course of a few days—I am very confident. time alone will determine the object.

I have Rec^d a hint from a friend that some Gentlemen of the Committee of Congress who were at Camp were not acquainted with the circumstances of the Court Martial held on me—and that some *Caitifs* had attempted to place it in a very unfavourable view. The whole of the proceedings are in the hands of Ric^d Peters Esqr. you will do me a particular favour to show it to some of these Gentlemen—for from [what] I can learn it has not been transmitted to Congress—altho' all Others are Regularly sent up.

The Difficulty I experience in prevented some Worthy Officers from Resigning (notwithstanding the *seven years half pay*) together with the Distress and real wants of the troops of this State has almost determined me to Retire to my *Sabine* field. Adieu, my Dear Sir & believe me yours most Sincerely

Source: *Pennsylvania Magazine of History and Biography* 11, no. 1 (1887): 115-16.
Delaney was a friend of Wayne's and a Colonel in the Pennsylvania Militia.

James Craik to Jonathan Potts

Dear Sir   Head Quarters, May 24, 1778
The Waggon arrived yesterday and the Waggoner has returned back to Reading as yet I have not got one—I observe my frind Bond has not Sent me any Bedding. so that I am affraid I shall be at a loss when we come to march—Several other things I gave him a memd. of are not yet come—I wish you could procure Some Cathartic Salts the Regimental Surgeons Complain greatly for want of them. You may engage any quantity at the Salt works in the Jersies—Sal: Nitri is much wanted and Cantharides—As the General has desired all the Orderly's to join their Regiments by the first of June and we have already had Some S[uffer]ing with Some of the Colos. about them. I wish some method could be fallen on to employ women that can be depended on The Genl. Says we may at least enlest them for the Same money that Soldiers are for he can no longer bear having an Army on paper and not have them to Act in the field—We still have fresh Accts. of the Enemy preparing to move Somewhere, and I believe they are going off they are putting their Horses on board, their Cannon & heavy Baggage, and they Seem to be in great Confusion in the City—By a Vessell in 2 days they say a French war is Dclared and that a fight has been betwixt the British & French Ships, in which Two of the British Ship were Sunk—I am dayly expecting the pleasure of Seeing you here. And very Respectfully Dr. Sir your Most obedt. hum. Set.

Source: *The New England Historical and Genealogical Register* 18 (January 1864): 34-35. Craik was Assistant Deputy Director of the Hospitals in the Middle Department. Potts was Deputy Director General of the Hospitals in the Middle Department, then based at Reading, Pennsylvania.

William Johnson to Allen McLane

Dear M^c.   Camp May 24th. 1778
I am going to scribble or word or two, I have spoke to the Genl. about what you spoke to me about and all is right the Genl.

Declares he would not do without you in the Light Corps no not for one 1000 Pound. Claypole will also go with him if he Chuses for news wee have non stiring but believe me Dear Capt. inviolabley Yours

Source: Allen McLane Papers, Manuscript Department, The New-York Historical Society.

John Chaloner to John Ladd Howell

Sir   Valley Forge 25th May 1778
    Yours to Col Blaine & myself, of the 24th Ins^t. receiv'd this Day. I shall see the Q M G, and do all I can with him, to promote a speedy removal of the Stores, from Elk, Charleston &ca, I have wrote C. H. to remove those most in value first—Thank you for your attention to this Business, continue pressing them to furnish you with Teams, & I shall Back your applications to the Q M G here, our joint exertions may produce some good, The Beef laid in for the Navy, should be sent on for the Army, if fit for use, I wish to have the Stores in your neighbourhood collected, and not to remain in their present scatter'd Condition I am D^r. Sir Your Very Hbl Servant.
Philadelphia will be ours in a few Days—You must inform Mr Huggins that He must in future receive all the Stores & provisions coming from the Southward & forward them to Camp—as Opportunity affords not failing to make proper application to the D Q M G for Teams Col Coxe & Petitt say they have orderd Col Hollingsworth and Wade to bend their whole force to your assistance

Source: Stewart Mss. 58.8, Rowan University Library. This was directed to Howell at Head of Elk, Maryland.

Alexander Scammell to Timothy Pickering

Dear Col^o Orderly Office May 26th 1778
    I acknowledge the Receipt of Y^r Letters of Y^e 3^d & 5th Ins^t. Mr St Clair went upon the Lines with Col^o Morgan a few Days, but soon got tir'd, and return'd—he appears very sensible, but seems to entertain too high a Notion for a Cadet at present—Indeed if he was

ever so fond of the Birth, I cant find any Col? willing to receive him into their Reg^{ts}. They say their pay wont admit of entertaining Cadets at their Table—I wish he may obtain a birth agreeable to his Merit, but doubt whether he will, The republican Jealousy so natural to americans, seems at present to run very high against Foreigners—I congratulate you on the pleasing Aspect of our Affairs, it would have given you the highest Satisfaction to have seen our great Genl enjoying the sublime Pleasure of a True Patriot (on the Day of rejoicing in Camp) encircled with all the Officers of his Army. Three Genl Discharges of Musketry, three times Thirteen Canon, besides three Huzzas to each Discharge, preceded the cold Collation, accompanied by a N? of Ladies—Numberless patriotic Toasts were drank on the Occasion—The Gen Joy seem'd to create a forgetfulness of past Toils & Fatigues—We considered ourselves upon the Scale of Nations We Look'd forward, we look'd round from The Atlantic, to the pacific Oceans travel'd from Darien to Baffin Bay—Look'd up to the rising Empire of America. Then look'd on the sparkling Glass, till balmy Sleep lock'd up our minds, employ'd in pleasing Dreams. then we dreamt of a N? of new Orders—Stars, Garters Laurels &c. &c. &c. &c. &c. But many of us awoke with violent Head Akes instead of new Titles, & upon the whole concluded; that a consciousness of having faithfully serv'd our struggling Country was superior to every outside Show, or empty Title—

That it is impossible to please every Body is verify'd by daily experience—Congress has fallen Short of pleasing the Officers in giving 7 Years ½ Pay. The more moderate say it is past their Expectation, and think it sufficient another Class say it would be best to have the seven years half pay paid at once. Others say they had rather have nothing—However all say they think it exceeding Hard, that the Widows & Families of Officers who should chance to be Kill'd in Action, or die before the Expiration of Y^e seven Years, should not be entitled to Y^e half pay—

The Enemy are manieuvring in Philadelphia the general Opinion is, that they are about leaving the City, that their Canon are on Board, sick & heavy Baggage. Their men are compleated with 40 Rounds of new Ammunition—many suppose they will cross jersey to south Amboy—which is probable—They may be attempting to draw us off our Ground—or occasion a Division of our Troops by Detachment & then fall upon us piece meal—If a french war is declar'd; probably they will retire, and collect their Forces to New

York—or be oblig'd to go to the west Indias—You may perhaps have heard that ye Marquis with 2000 men had like to have been cut off by the enemy, who march'd out in full strength to the N^o of 10,000, by all we can collect—turn'd the Flank of the Marquis body, and got quite in his Rear, and had Genl Grant push'd as he easily might have done, the whole party must have been either kill'd or taken—But to the disgrace of Y^e british Army they permited the Party to cross Matsons Ford in sight of them, and scarcely a man of ours kill'd wounded or made prisoner—Our Indians had a curious fray with an equal number of light Horse, kill'd and wounded say 15—& drove them off terribly frightened with the War Hoop—About 40 of the enemy were kill'd, wounded, made prisoners & deserted—By depending on the Militia to guard the passes of their left, the enemy stole the march upon our Party—Taking a very circuitous Rout—May 27nd The last Reports from the City say that all the enemy's Baggage, a Reg^t of their Horse—all the women & Children, Together with the Tories, and their Effects and all our poor Soldiers prisoners with them, are put on board Ship—The latter in Irons—Although Genl Green has done every thing possible in his Department, the short time he has been in it; Yet you can easily judge; that we are by no means compleated for a Movement. When I look back to last Winter, I'll assure you it makes one shudder a Want of Magazines of Provisions, bad Traveling and several unlucky Circumstances nearly starv'd our Army—The QMG^{ls} Department was a <u>Vox & preterea Nihil</u>—But my Indignation burns, when I reflect on the criminal Neglect of the Clothier—It is the Opinion of our best Surgeons, that we lost near a Thousand men for the want of Cloathes only when a plenty was in the Country. his neglect must therefore be unpardonable And the Lives of so many brave Americans lost through his Neglect, laid to his Charge—a heavy one indeed. We have with the utmost difficulty trac'd the Box so much sought after, to Mr Hooper, Mr Weis is ready to be qualify'd that he deliverd it with his own Hands to Hooper, & told him the Contents. Hooper I understand pretends that he knows nothing of the matter and that he does'nt recollect any thing about it—The Genl is determin'd to have a strict Enquiry made into it. But I am fearfull it is lost irrecoverably—My next perhaps will be dated in Philadelphia, or Hudsons River—Tho they give out, that they shall Attempt to carry out Lines & if they fail Y^e Attempt they shall burn all before them. But I believe their Threats, as little as I fear their Attempt—The Officers are anxious about the New Arrangement, I wish it might soon take place or be totally laid aside, for this Campaign, that they might know what to depend upon You ask'd my Opinion, concerning the practicability of lopping off the Excrescencies of those Gentlemen's Riches, who have been amassing Wealth to the prejudice of our Currency, and contrary to every principle of Honesty. I wish it could be put in Execution; but am apprehensive, that men of that Kidney would compose a great Majority of No^s.—When the Din of War ceases, and we can have a breathing spell, I hope Justice, & Equity will take the place of Rapine & Extortion. Y^r. sincere Friend & very Humle Servt

NB I send enclos'd seven Dollars, which you had deliver'd an Officer in Genl Varnums Brigade for the use of the Brigade for the use of the sick—I forget his Name—

The retreat across Schuylkill did great Credit to the Marquis & his Officers—The men kept their ranks in perfect order, even whilst fording the River, & form'd on the west Side with great Expedition.

Source: Timothy Pickering Papers, Massachusetts Historical Society.
Scammell was describing the *Feu de Joie* on May 6, and Lafayette's "Barren Hill Expedition."

John Cropper Jr. to Peggy Cropper

My Dear Peggy,   Camp Valley Forge, 29th. May 1778
        Having a favorable opportunity I do myself the pleasure of writing you as fully as possible, and must beg your patience and attention.—You are much surpris'd, and I'm afraid unhappy that I've disappointed in my several promises to come home from time to time; nor do I wonder at your surprise, neither shou'd I think strange if you believ'd it my intention never to come home; for I have deceiv'd myself, and wou'd not have believ'd an angel, if he'd told me that I shou'd have stay'd so long from the arms of my <u>dear wife</u>, my <u>darling infant</u>, and the management of my unsettled estate at home—but, so it is,—and as sure as there is a god in heaven, or that you and I exist, my motives are laudible, and my intentions innocent—Let it be sufficient for the present to say, that the exigency of my country's cause, my over fondness for a military profession, and the advice of those I esteem my friends, have so long kept me from the enjoyment of domestick happiness, with an <u>amiable wife</u>, delightful <u>little daughter</u>, and <u>social</u>

friends. It is with the greatest reluctance I stay in camp, when I consider what you suffer in my absence—but, my country's call, the greatest of all calls, demands my presence with the army for a time, to pay for the blessings I have enjoy'd, and expect to enjoy under the auspices of Liberty.—My dear, when you consider my conduct since our first acquaintance—when you consider I was faithful & constant at a time when I might have ruin'd your reputation forever—when you consider I marry'd you ag^t. the will & consent of not only my father & mother, but ag^t. the advice and persuasion of all those who call'd themselves my friends—When you reflect upon those considerations, for which I dont pretend to claim the smallest merit; I hope; I beg you by the remembrance of the pleasures we have enjoy'd together, to content yourself untill next fall; as the spouse of him who is serving the cause of his country, himself, and every thing that can be near & dear: But, if you think you cannot wait 'till that time, that it will destroy your happiness, inform me by Lieu^t. Custis, and I will (however disagreeable it may be), resign immediately upon his return—

The campain is now begun, and I am desirous to see the end of it—By those who came last from Virginia, indeed I was inform'd before, that there was a misunderstanding between you & Uncle Corbin, for which I am excessive sorry—I am afraid you've been mis inform'd, or misled by some of your friends—I'm afraid M^r. Abbott is to blame for this—be it as it will, I beseech you to loose no time in making it up, for I cannot be happy while there is any difference between you & him—I have wrote to him very fully on the subject, & positively insisted to have it made up, and said I was shure you'd not be against it.—I beg you to be satisfy'd my dear, that I never promis'd you to come home, or indeed made any other promise, but what as the time I intended to perform, and be satisfy'd that however strange my conduct may have appear'd, that is has ever been for the honor & happiness of my family. Lieut^t. Custis who has stay'd with me several days, since his escape from the Enemy, waits upon you with this, who is & has been my good friend: From him you may learn of my situation & my intentions.—I send you one peice of linen ab^t. 20 yds. coarse, also one half peice and 2 ½ yds of superfine, ab^t. 13 yds wraped up in two new shirts, which I drew from the Continental store, but they are so badly made, as you will see, that they are not fit to wear till made over again—Also 3 pr stockings, two of which I had made at Bethlehem, & send them home to be whitened; the other pair are yours, which I dont want as I have stockings enough to last me till next winter—also 1 pr of leather shoes made at Bethlehem, I am afraid they are too Small, and am certain they are very homely ones—One pr of black Shammy do flower'd, done at Bethlehem—I send you a plain gold ring, which if you please present to our good Sister, & request her to wear it until I return—it is like yours sent by Lieut^t. Kindall. The fine linen Sent down is for yourself—I want the two Shirts made over again & ruffled, also 6 Shirts made of the coarse linen & ruffled w^t. fine cambrick if possible to be got—When Lieut Custis returns to camp, you will please send me two or three Shirts & Stocks, and if you've any stuff for Summer waistcoats & breeches—Lieut. Custis will also bring up my horse & watch—

I shou'd be extreemely glad to See our brother Wm Pettit at camp; if he will come up, he will be at no expense while he stays in camp—at any rate I shou'd be glad to See any one that cou'd give an acc^t. of my affairs.—I particularly request you to write me by next opportunity with your own hand—and recommend you to practice reading & writing 'till I return home My Dear Peggy, I am your sincere & ever faithfull husband

Source: Mortimer Rare Book Room, Smith College, Northampton, Massachusetts. Cropper, Lieutenant Colonel of the Eleventh Virginia Regiment, was writing to his wife in Accomac County, Virginia.

Tench Tilghman to James Tilghman

Hon^d. Sir   Head Quarters Valley Forge 31st. May 1778.
I recd. yours by General Cadwalader and by Genl. Dickinson. I cannot say they gave me pleasure because at the time of writing them you seem to have been under very great uneasiness.—I will not undertake to dictate, but I wish for your own sake, that of your family, and the preservation of your fortune, you would think seriously of conforming to the law of the Country in which you are obliged to live in. If you thought the Measures which have been pursued, wrong, you have done everything in your power to oppose them, not by acting, but by speaking your sentiments moderately and in such a manner, that even those of a different opinion have not blamed you. A Majority of people upon this Continent are determined to support the independency of America, and a great European Power has acknowledged and determined also to support them in it. Great Britain

has herself in fact acknowledged the independency, for Sir Henry Clinton has this day informed the General that he is charged with dispatches from Lord Howe the Kings Commissioner to Congress. What these dispatches contain I do not know. But formerly they foolishly disdained to mention the name of Congress but in the most contemptuous manner. Things being thus circumstanced, it is no more derogatory to your honour an Conscience to take an Oath of fidelity to the form of Government under which you live, that it is for a Member of any representative Body to take an Oath which he had opposed in the House. He takes it because the Majority think it right—A few days ago M^r. Secretary Matlock inclosed me your parole, and desired me to forward it to you, informing you that you were discharged from it and at liberty to act as you should judge best. I take it for granted that you have seen the law of the State of Pennsylvania which affects you, but lest you should not, I inclose you a single sheet which has the two material sections N°. 8 and 9. As you are out of the province, you may take time to consider well of it, and if you chuse to conform, which I hope in God you will, you may do it any time within ten days after you come in. The folly of the British Ministry in sending out terms after they knew we had concluded an Alliance with France, crowns all their former acts of Madness. The terms of our Alliance with France are generous to the highest degree, we are not even bound to give them an exclusive trade. We only engaged to assist them should they be drawn into a War with England on our Account. You always treated my intelligence of the intentions of france as chimerical. I could not speak plainer than I did consistent with my duty and the confidence reposed in me. But you may be assured, that not only France but the whole of her Connection are determined to support America ag^t. Great Britain and whether she will be able to overpower us backed by such powerful Advocates you may judge from the Struggles we have heretofore made alone—The British Army leave Philad^a. in a few days and leave hundreds to curse the wretched Situation into which they are drawn. They must stay exposed to the Resentment of their Countrymen, or go, dependent on those who care not for them. I do not certainly know who of my former friends intend to remain. Andrew Allen takes his family with him. T. Coxe I am told intends to stay and take his chance. Many have came out and taken the Oaths. M^r. Physick was here to-day and took them. M^r. Chew I am told intends to do the same, but I only have it from report. I do not well understand the nature of my Brother

James's case. If by his parole he is bound to return when called upon, he cannot with any propriety be asked to give any kind of information respecting what he saw while in the hands of the Enemy, either respecting the persons or any other Matter. But if his parole was barely to remain at home and not bear Arms during this War, he is only bound to do that. The State have a right to call upon him to give Evidence or to do any other duty in common with other Citizens— These are the rules of Parole in the Army, and I believe what ought to govern every where else—A great quantity of Goods will be left in Philad^a. and there you may supply yourself in a few days. You cannot make use of the mode you propose, I know Officers and others get them out of town but then it is ag^t. orders and if they are found out the Goods are confiscated and the persons punished. Your letter shall be sent to T. Coxe. Let matters get a little settled and I will engage to bring my rash and childish Brother home in safety provided he will return—surely he will not wish to remain in a Service, in which, void of friends to push his future he may obtain a Lieutenancy at the end of his life. His was the inconsiderate action of a Boy and as such I dare say I can get it overlooked, provided he does not persevere till he becomes a Man. I write in haste and incoherently. We are busy in preparing to march to the North River. The British Army goes first to New York, ours of course will be near them—Ten Regiments go to Jamaica—perhaps they may be too late—I shall not be surprised if all the Troops leave the Continent to save the Islands. France has ten thousand Men there ready to strike. I speak not vaguely. I know it as certainly, as I know the Returns of our own Army. You must make my excuses to M^r. Earle, my Sisters and Billy for not writing to them. In fact I have not time. When we are fixed again, you shall hear from me, and have my opinions upon the operations of the Campaign. I imagine at present it will be a quiet one. The British Army in New York will be too strongly posted to attack, and if they detatch to the West Indies they will be too weak to attack us. Adieu my dear and honoured Sir and believe me, your truly Affec^t. Son

Source: *Memoir of Lieut. Col. Tench Tilghman, Secretary and Aid to Washington, Together With an Appendix, containing Revolutionary Journals and Letters, Hitherto Unpublished* (Albany: J. Munsell, 1876), 167-70.

Jedediah Huntington to Andrew Huntington

Dear Sir—   Valley Forge 2ᵈ June
    We are here still althou' we have been under marching Orders several Days—as the Enemy have been continualy at Work in Preparations to leave the City for a Month or more we must believe they are near or quite ready—
    if they go the NYork as we expect—we should take our Course that Way—they would I dare say be glad to see us divide here that they might attack us in Part—but we shall not give them the Opportunity—Our Army is in such Condition and Numbers that we would gladly meet then with our whole strength—
    There has been great Plenty of Rain in these Parts since last Sunday Week—the Apple Bloom here & in Jersey was good—my Love to Sister &C—I remain your affectionate Broʳ.

Source: Huntington Papers, The Connecticut Historical Society.

Dudley Colman to Mrs. Colman

My Dear   Camp Valley Forge June 4ᵗʰ. 1778
    I had the Pleasure of a Letter from you by Colᵒ Wigglesworth Saturday Night last it is a little Strange You had recᵈ no Letters from me as I have sent several—We have been Under Marching orders these 10 Days as we hourly expect the News that the Enemy have left the City of Philaᵃ it is probable we shall in a few Days be nearer New England Nothing particular has happened lately except a Spy being executed this Morning he was an Officer in the 10ᵗʰ. Pennsylvania Regᵗ. & was Discharged last Decʳ. for Stealing 2 pʳ. of Shoes he Stole a Horse & went into the City & last Tuesday came out as a Spy & was taken up & this Morning hang'd—I recᵈ. the things You sent by Colˡ Wigglesworth please to present my best Regards to Mʳˢ. Giddings—by the best Accounts the Enemy have embarked all their Stores & Artillery & we expect are going thro' the Jerseys to New York with their Troops the next Opportunity of writing to You I hope will be that Way In the mean Time I wish You Health & hope that the Affairs of our Country will take so happy a turn that we may have an Opportunity of seeing each other in Peace give my best Compliments

to all enquiring Friends love to little Bridget &c I am my Dear Your best Husband

PS: You may tell M^r. Enoch Ro[sse] that I have the Unhappiness to send him the News that his son Richard a few Days ago Deserted to the Enemy—Billy desires to be remembered to You

Source: Dudley Colman Papers, Massachusetts Historical Society.
Colman, also spelled Coleman, was Lieutenant Colonel of the Thirteenth Massachusetts Regiment. Thomas Shanks, formerly an Ensign in the Tenth Pennsylvania, was convicted by a Board of General Officers for being a spy, and executed on June 4, 1778.

Charles Lee to Benjamin Rush

My Dr Rush,   Camp at Valley forge June ye 4th 1778.
Tho I had no occasion for fresh assurances of your Friendship, I cannot help being much pleased with the warmth of your letter, deliver'd to me by M^r. Hale, breathes, and I hope it is unnecessary to assure you that my sentiments with respect to you, are correspondent—You would think it odd that I shou'd seem to be an Apologist for General Howe. I know not how it happens, but when I have taken prejudices in favor or against a Man, I find a difficulty in shaking them off—From my first acquaintance with M^r. Howe I lik'd him I thought him friendly candid good natur'd brave and rather sensible than the reverse. I believe still that he is naturally so, but a corrupt or more properly speaking no education, the fashion of the times, the reigning idolatry among the English (particularly the soldiery) for every scepter'd Calf, Wolf, Hog, or Ass, have so totally perverted his understanding and heart, that private friendship has not force sufficient to keep a door open for the admittance of mercy for political Hereticks. He was besides perswaded that I was doubly criminal both as Traitor and Deserter—in short so totally was He inebriated with this idea that I am convinced He wou'd have thought himself both politically and morally damn'd had he acted any part than what He did—He is besides the most indolent of Mortals, never took farther pains to examine the merits or demerits of the Cause in which He was engaged than merely to recollect that Great Britain was said to be the Mother Country, George the Third King of Great Britain, that the Parliament was call'd the representatives of G. Britain, that the King and Parliament form'd the Supreme Power, that

a Supreme Power is absolute and incontrollable, that all resistance must consequently be rebellion, but above all that He was a Soldier, and bound to obey in all cases whatsoever—these are his notions, and this his logic, but through these absurdities I cou'd distinguish when He was left to himself rays of Friendship and good nature breaking out—it is true that he was seldom left to himself, for never poor Mortal thrust into high stations, was surrounded by such fools and scoundrels—MᶜKensey, Balfour, Galoway were his Councillors— They urg'd him to all his acts of harshness. They were his Scribes; all the damn'd stuff which was issued to the astonish'd World was theirs—I believe He scarcely ever read the letters He signed—You will scarcely believe it, but I can assure you as a fact, that He never read that curious proclamation issued at the Head of Elk, till three days after it was publish'd—You will say that I am drawing my Friend Howe in more ridiculous colours than He has yet been represent'd in—but this is his real character—He is naturally good humour'd and complacent, but illiterate and indolent to the last degree unless as an executive Soldier, in which capacity He is all fire and activity, brave and cool as Julius Caesar—his understanding is, as I observ'd before rather good than otherwise, but was totally confounded and stupefy'd by the immensity of the task impos'd upon him—He shut his eyes, fought his battles, drank his bottle, had his little Whore, advis'd with his Counsellors, receiv'd his orders from North and Germain, one more absurd than the other, took Galoways opinion, shut his eyes, fought again, and is now I suppose to be call'd to Account for acting according to instructions; but I believe his eyes are now open'd. He sees that He has been an instrument of wickedness and folly—indeed when I observ'd it to him, He not only patiently took the observation, but indirectly assented to the truth of it—He made at the same time as far as his *mauvaise honte* wou'd permit an apology for his treatment of me—Thus far with regard to Mʳ Howe—You are struck with the great events, changes and new characters which have appear'd on the stage since I saw you last—but I am more struck with the Admirable efficacy of Blunder—it seem'd to be a tryal of skill which Party shou'd outdoe the other, and it is hard to say which play'd the deepest strokes—but it was a capital one of ours which certainly gave the happy turn which affairs have taken. Upon my Soul it was time for fortune to interpose or We were inevitably lost—but this we will talk over another time—I suppose we

shall see one another at Philadelphia very soon—*en attendant*—God
bless you Yours affectionately
My love to Mrs Rush

Source: *The Lee Papers,Vol 2: 1776-1778, Collections of the New-York Historical
Society For the Year 1872*(New York: The Society, 1873), 397-99.

Jedediah Huntington to Andrew Huntington

Dear Sir   Valley Forge 5th June 1778
          Just as I was coming out of Norwich Peter Plumb produced
me a Certificate from Doctor Turner purporting that he was unfit for
Duty in Camp but was able to work at his Trade. I trouble you with
an order for him to apply to Q^r Mr Hubbard at Hartford or to Col Hay
D Q M G at Fish Kill to be employed by them wish You to send it to
him & inform me whether he is gone in your next.
          7th Mr Loring Com^y of Prisoners officially informed us the
Day before yesterday that the Army was about to leave Philad^a. that
Genl Clinton did not wish to carry off the Prisoners of War but would
send them out to us or leave them in the City provided we would
promise to let them have as many in Exchange at some other Time.
          Sunday Evening.   The Commissioners are arrived in
Philadelphia. Governor Johnstone, Earl of Carlisle & Mr Eden a
Brother of the late Governor Eden Lord Howe & Genl Clinton are the
other two. Lord Cornwallis is returned. whether their Arrival will
delay the Army leaving Philad^a or not a few Days will discover.
please to give my Love to sister. from you affect Bro^r
          Great Numbers of Recruits have come in from Maryland &
the Jersies. their Regiments will outnumber ours. those from
Maryland are for the War. There has been a rebellious Rising in one
of the Counties in England in Opposition to the raising of Recruits for
the american War. give my Love to Thos Fanning & tell him I will
write him in a few Days about his Ration Acc^o sent to Major Alden.

Source: Huntington Papers, The Connecticut Historical Society.

Eleazer Oswald to John Lamb

Dear Colonel,   Artillery Park Valley Forge, 7 June 1778

I was in Hopes to have had the Pleasure of seeing you in this Quarter 'ere This—But I imagine I shall not have that Satisfaction, till a Junction of our Army, which I suppose will very shortly take place, as we have been under marching Orders this Week past. I myself am under marchg Orders with 8 Pieces of artillery & 4 Companies to join the Right Wing of the Army commanded by Genl. Lee, who is first to move off the Ground in the Disposition of March.

The Enemy, its generally believed, will leave the City of Phil^a. in a day or two, part of them with upwards of 200 Waggons are now in Jersey near Cooper's Ferry, all their Transports &c are down below Billings port, at Reedy Island. Tho' notwithstanding all this some are of Opinion that they are yet determined to attack us, or manouv[er] us off the Ground.—

This morning we received in Camp the inclosed Establishment of our Army, and take the Earliest Opportunity to transmit it to you. Our Friend Cri[ms]hier goes to the "right a bout," unless a Commission can be given him;—Serjeant Cunningham is appointed Serj^t: Major to your Regiment—as he has acted in that Capacity ever since the Battalion was first raised, and as I believe you are sensible it is his Right, you will approve of the Appointment. he is certainly one of the best Serjeants in the Corps—steady & attention to his Duty—and in my Opinion would execute the Duties of a Commission equal to many who now hold that honor. While we have been in the Park some one or other of the L^{ts}. have done adjutants Duty P.T. for which they have received pay, but this will be no hindrance to M^r. Hubble's being confirmed as Adjutant to the Battalion,—Col^o. Harrison with his Reg^t. are arrived in the Park, they are all raw & inexperienced, yet from priority of Commissions claim the right of being the first Battalion—their Commissions they say are dated in Novr. 1776, when Congress ordered the Battalion to be raised, but as those who have been in (& seen more) Service longer, deny the Right on Principles of Justice & Reason, we parade Regimentally. I suppose the Rank will not be settled till we all join, which Event I flatter my self is not far distant; indeed, were you & Col^o Crane present Genl. Knox would request a Board of General Officers for that purpose, as he told me the other Day your being Absent was the only Reason why he declined it. At the same Time he hinted to me that he sincerely wished it may fall to your Lot to have the precedency of the other Colonels, and assigned many judicious Reasons for it.

Generals Arnold & Knox, together with many Gentlemen of our Corps desire their Regards to you. Please to give my Respects to all the Gentlemen of our Acquaintance, in your Department, and believe me, Dr Colonel, Yours sincerely

Source: John Lamb Papers, Manuscript Department, The New-York Historical Society. Oswald was a Lieutenant Colonel in the Second Artillery Regiment.

Richard Peters to Timothy Pickering

My Dear Sir   Head Q^{rs}. 7th. June 1778

I arrived here Yesterday—I find a great Variety of Reports prevailing but they all tend to prove the Enemy's Intention to evacuate the City—When this Event will happen is not certain but it is generally expected every Moment—The Commissioners are arrived & Lord Cornwallis with them. It is said a Reinforcement came with them but their Number not ascertained. It is not believed to be of great Consequence as to Number. Loring is full freighted with & told Mr Boudinot at a Meeting they had on the Lines yesterday a quantum suff^y. of Lies. Such as that, the American Commissioners in France were sent from that Court with Disgrace & might speedily be expected at New York. That of Course France had rescinded all her Proceedings as to us &c &c. This he told seriously to Mr Boudinot & seemed to be Fool enough to believe it. The British Army would have gone before this Time as it appears they have had Orders for this Purpose & were prepared for there Departure but on the Arrival of the Com^{rs} the Orders were countermanded as Deserter just come in informs. I fancy a Delay of a few Days will ensue from the Arrival of the Com^{rs}. but I cannot believe that so great a military Movement will be totally stopped as no uncommon Circumstances could have happened in Europe since our last Accounts—It is certain all their Ships except the Vigilant & one other are below the Chevaux de frize & great Part of the Army in the Jerseys opposite the City. They have destroyed all supernumerary Provisions & even Blanketts & every thing they thought could be serviceable to us. It is said great Numbers have applied for Passages more than could obtain them—The Multitude of Proscriptions alarms even the lowest among the Tories

& I fear that we shall lose a Number of useful Mechanics who would have been good Subjects notwithstanding any Part their Fears prompted them to take with the Enemy during the Operation of the first Impression made by the Enemy's possessing the City. I wish this Matter had been better considered & that all our Governments would act upon the great Scale in this as well as every other Business.

I am very much pleased at the Appearance of Reformation I perceive in the Army in almost every other particular but Clothing. Linnen they are in great Need of & every possible Method should be taken to procure it. Shirts particularly—However they are much better than I expected in this Respect.

I do not write to Mrs Peters because I think she is on her Journey to her Mothers. If anything should have delayed it I expect she will inform me. I will wait a few Days for the Motions of the Enemy & if I see no Probability of their moving I will go round thro' Chester County & share your Toils. I hope you are at my House. Remember me dutifully to my Mother & affectionately to Duer & all Friends.

Loring told Boudinot that the Portsmouth Frigate was captured. I am with great Sincerity your affectionate

Bob Smith has some Company Accts to settle to & intends for York [ ]eadily

The Commissioners are Lord Carlisle Govr Johnstone W. Eden Esqr. Brother of Govr Eden

Source: Timothy Pickering Papers, Massachusetts Historical Society.
Peters was Secretary of the Board of War which had been meeting in York, Pennsylvania. He shows the expectations of many, that the British Army would soon evacuate Philadelphia.

Alexander Scammell to Allen McLane

Dear Sir—   June 9^{nth} 78
I shall send you a relief of picked men the time you request. I congratulate you upon your success in surprizing the enemy, when the Odds was so much against you—At the particular request of Lt Stoy, backed by his Col^o, I gave him a pass for 3 or 4 days, to procure Evidence, it being a piece of Politeness due every Officer in his Situation. More especially as he has been in Arrest so long—I should

had sent for you, and your Evidence against him before this time, could you been spared from the Lines. If you will appoint a Day, and give me Notice, when you think you can conveniently leave the Lines and attend the Court, I will order the Court to sit accordingly—The Carabine taken, and sent to my Office belongs to your Party—If you will send an Order by any of your men I ll give them the money for them I am Y^r Most Obed^t Servt

Source: Allen McLane Papers, Manuscript Department, The New-York Historical Society.

Richard Peters to Timothy Pickering

My dear Sir   Head Q^{rs}. June 9th. 1778
        I received yours relative to your Bundle which Col Scammell has & which I intended to have sent to Col. Slough at Lanc^r. but finding two Light Horsemen intending to return to York Col Scammel has concluded that it will be best to send it by them. The Army will shortly move. I believe in a Day or two & this weighed in our Councils held on your Goods & Chattles. There is no News of any Consequence I am happy to hear that Congress in their Answer to Lord Howe & Genl Clinton have anticipated anything the Commissioners have to say unless they choose to do the only Thing which will save their Nation from Perdition—acknowledge our Independence & make Peace.
        I am much obliged by your Information of a Visit to my Family & have anxiously waited for a Letter from M^{rs}. Peters informing me certainly when she would proceed on her Journey. I will not wait here longer than tomorrow when if I do not hear of something decisive I will go, by the Way of Nottingham, Home where I feel very desirous to arrive not only on my own but your Account as I fear you have your Hands too full but hope M^r. Smith will be able to assist you in the executive Part. I took my ride in Time for I have felt a small Return of my bilious Complaint of which I now perfectly free owing to the Exercise.
        I continue to be pleased with the Appearance of everything here. Discipline seems to be growing apace & America will be under lasting Obligations to the Baron Steuben as the Father of it. He is much respected by the Officers & beloved by the Soldiers who

themselves seem to be convinced of the Propriety & Necessity of his Regulations. I am astonished at the Progress he has made with the Troops.

The Army is in general well armed save that they want a great Number of Bayonets which I think ought to be sent them. As it Cloathing I can say but few pleasing Things on that Score. Shirts are distressingly wanted. Their Nastiness & of Course Want of Health in this Respect exceeds Description. I wish Materials for making Shirts & Overalls were sent to every Regiment to be made up by their own Taylors. This is really an Object of the first Consequence as a Soldier can never be healthy who is not nor can keep himself clean. The Surgeons think we have lost at least one thousand Men merely for Want of Changes of Linnen. I find great Numbers of the Officers object to Hunting Shirts & would rather have a short Waistcoat with Sleeves. They say a trifling Shower wets a Man thro' immediately & wet Linnen is much worse than wet woolen. I do not hear of any of our Tools being distributed except a few Needles. I believe it will be a Week before I can reach York & by that Time I am of Opinion notwithstanding other People differ with me that we shall have Possession of Philadelphia. I am with great Regard your afft. hble Serv

Remember me to my Mother. I suppose Saley to be at her Brothers & therefore do not write.

Congress now stands high with the Army who are in general well pleased with the Establishment & the late Regulations.

Source: Timothy Pickering Papers, Massachusetts Historical Society.

Clement Biddle to Moore Furman

Dear Sir   Camp Valley Forge June 10, 1778

Since I wrote you last the Arrival of Commissioners from England at Philadelphia with Lord Cornwallis (but no reinforcements) has retarded the Enemies departure & leaves us in suspense—Altho' it may delay them a short Time I think they proceed on their former plan and I would by all means have the quantities of Forage kept up to serve for a sudden march of our Army through Jersey and the directions heretofore given fully attended to—I have already mentiond the propriety of keeping no more Forage on the Line from

Trenton Landing to Brunswick than is Absolutely necessary for the Occasional use of the post & Cavalry—the same on the route from Coopers Ferry to South Amboy as the Enemy in Case they march thro' Jersey may probably take these routes—

A prize Brig taken & brought into Egg harbour has 5000 bushel Oats & about 1200 bags—I have engaged it & sent Col°. Lawrence & thro' him to Mr Ball 14.400 Dollars to pay for the same & Carriage I have directed that Col° Lawrence sends down Corn to supply the Waggons hawling from Egg harbour—which are to bring back loads of Oats to be lodged at Pennington or some place not it too great Quantities 6 to 10 miles North of the Princeton Road for security—I wish as little as possible of this Oats to be used at present intending it for the Cavalry wherever we may be in the months of July & August & the bags are not to be delivered out on Any Account but by my Order as I want them for a special purpose—I have wrote this to Col°. Lawrence—

I wish all returns could be completed to the 1st. of June or Orderd to be done the 1st. July as you find most Convenient.—

If we should remove towards the North River how is Bergen County stockd with Grain—it yields great quantities—

Dont let us fail on the routes as I fully expect we shall remove before a week—

This comes by Mr John Myers—he is an Inhabitant of Jersey who has been some time employ'd in the Army & is strongly recommended to me for a birth—he is desirous of a place in Jersey as his Family is there, therefore I recommend him to you—if any Employment can be found for him there

An Exchange of Prisoners is agreed on I am Dr Sir Y^r Obed h^l Serv

I have let M^r. Ludwick have 500 D^s. more & charged to you—how much am I to pay him on your Account.

Source: Record Group: Department of Defense; Subgroup: Revolutionary War; Mss. 4673, Division of Archives and Records Management, New Jersey State Archives.

Peter Grubb to Allen McLane

Dear McLane,   Camp 10th. May[sic] 1778
I rec^d. your Letter by McCulloch—I find the Enemy are still in possession of the City but cannot help think they would have Evacuated,

had not the Commissioners arived which in all probability will detain them some Time longer—last night arived at Head Quarters a Letter from those respectable People which I'm informed contains something concerning a Treaty—God grant it may contain such Terms as we can agree to—

Shou'd they continue one week longer many Beaver Hatts will be lost—The Whole Army this day moves to Ground where they will Encamp—A Committee from Congress is arived to setle the Arrangement of the Army—two Months Pay is drawn for our Division and our Men are constantly Drunk & with difficulty we can get ten Men on Parade—Co^l. Parke is restored to his Command—I am D^r. S^r. Y^r. Affect. F^d. & Hbl Sr^t.

Source: Allen McLane Papers, Manuscript Department, The New-York Historical Society. Grubb, a Captain in Patton's Additional Regiment, misdated this letter. The references to moving the camp and the peace commissioners, date this letter to June 10, not May 10, 1778.

Francis Johnston to George Washington

Sir,   Camp Mount Joy June 11. 1778

I beg leave to inform Your Excellency that the Bearer Capt. Kimmell, Pay Master to my Reg^t, is under the necessity of leaving the service—a thing extremely disagreeable to him; but such is the peculiar situation of his affairs in Consequence of his father's death, that he cannot possibly avoid it.

Lieut. Vernon of my Reg^t. with Y^r Excellency's approbation will act in Mr Kimmell's room. Should Your Excellency approve of him, it perhaps would not be improper to put it in orders, otherwise the Pay Master Genl will not furnish him with any cash on the Abstracts he shall deliver in.

Mr Kimmell means to remain on this ground till all his accounts are settled. I have the honor to be Y^r Excellency's most obed^t.

Source: George Washington Papers, Roll 49, Library of Congress.
Johnston was Colonel of the Fifth Pennsylvania.

Dudley Colman to Mrs. Colman

My Dear   Camp Valley Forge June 12th: 1778
        I wrote You a few Days ago by Lieu^t. Criqui in which I informed You that we were under marching Orders supposing the Enemy were about quitting the City of Phila^a. but since that the Comissioners have arrived from England Viz Lord Carlisle, Govr. Johnston & Mr Eden by whose coming I suppose their evacuating the City is delayed & it is uncertain whether we shall remove from this Part of the Country or not however a few Days will determine we are now encamped in the Field within a Mile of our Huts which we moved out of, the Day before Yesterday, for the Benefit of the Air—I have Just now seen a Man by the Name of Lemuel Collins belonging to Cape Ann who has been taken a Prisoner & is returning Home from Carolina he informs me that Capt. Jon^a. Parsons came from Carolina in the Vessell with him having arrived there after he had been taken Prisoner Nathl. Jones came from Carolina to Virginia with Capt Parsons but Capt Parsons could not prevail with him to come farther this Way he has entered on board a Vessell in Virginia he had the Misfortune to lose all his Cloaths in the Fire at Charlestown but has about 3 or 400 Dollars Prize Money due in Carolina for his last Cruise which I understand he has given Capt Parsons orders about Capt. Parsons is going to the West Indies in a small Schooner from Virginia I have nothing of News to write You please to give my best Compliments to all enquiring Friends my Love to little Bridget I am my Dear Your Affectionate Husband
P:S: I have sent by Mr Bishop of Mistick by whom this goes three Hundred Dollars—what You dont want for Yourself of it You may pay Capt Wyer with it give my best Regards likewise to his Brother Tim—

Source: Dudley Colman Papers, Masschusetts Historical Society.

John Conway to William Maxwell

Sir   Camp, Valley forge, 12th. June,—78.
        By M^r: Samuel Caldwell, conductor of Waggons I send you sundries as p^r: the inclosed invoice.—The Arms are mostly French & Hessian, one box only of British. I stript the store to get them & am sorry there was no better on hand. There is not a tent in the store, nor

a cartouch box; I drew 250 canisters as a substitute 'till they can be got.—

M^r: Weiss had packed up some bell tents in a large box, but they could not be carried; he has given me a form of a return, which is inclos^d & which he requests may be made use of in future. when tents &ca: come in he promises to forward them to the Brigade.—Our Army has left the huts & encamped about 3 mile in front, their movement has delayed my business, & given me a great deal of trouble.—

I set out to Morrow Morning for Lancaster.

Kettles must be drawn at the Manufactory near Mount Holly, Genl. Green will send an order for as many as the Brigade wants. I am Sir,y^r: Most Ob^dt. serv.

Source: Shreve Papers, Department of Special Collections, Manuscripts and Archives, Prescott Memorial Library, Louisiana Tech University, Lamar, Louisiana. Conway was Major of the Fourth New Jersey Regiment.

John Laurance to Timothy Pickering

Dear Sir   Camp Valley Forge June 13th 1778

I was from Camp, on a Visit to my Family, when your Letter of June 3^d reached it. On my return I had the pleasure of receiving it—The Disappointment gives me no other concern, than its depriving me of the pleasure of being near you; for, on the whole, in point of Interest my present Office is preferable—You will be pleased to accept of my Hands for the trouble you have taken respecting the Affair—

I have sent, from time to time, under cover to the Secretary of your Board the Proceedings of Courts Martial, that have been held in the Army, during the Winter; with a request he would mention the receipt of them—will you be so good as to acquaint me Whether they were received, and Whether you have heard any thing respecting those that were sent away with your Papers. I would also be obliged to you to inform me the Names of the Gentlemen who constitute the Continental Navy Board, as I want to write to them respecting the affairs of a Young Gentleman, who was left in the *Randolph* Frigate to whom I was related. These favours must be added to the Account you have against me, and when a suitable Opportunity offers I must endeavour to discharge it—I Am with much Regard Your obliged serv

Source: Timothy Pickering Papers, Massachusetts Historical Society.

Alexander Scammell to Timothy Pickering

Dear Sir— Orderly Office June 14th—78

Yours of the 4 & 6th Instant have come to hand, I have deliver'd the ten Dollars to Mr St Clair—He seems desirous of entering one of the Regts of Horse, have recommended him to Major Clough, to procure a Birth for him as Cadet in the Regt to which he belongs—He has been on the Lines with McLane this fortnight past—I wish he may innure himself to fatigues, and wear off that inactivity & Supiness so natural to him—He is Shiftless, I sincerely pity him—And am dispos'd to assist him all that lays in my power. I beg you would not give yourself the least Uneasiness in supposing, that St Clair by reason of Yr Letter has been burthensome to me—(Tho I should ever be happy in looking upon & treating every Gentleman recommended or acquainted with Colo Pickering as my own Friends-) As I was inclind upon first hearing his Story, to compassionate, & befriend him—

The Bundle sent on by your better half I have by advice of Mr Peters confided to Mr Blaine's Care, to transmit to Yorktown which he has promis'd to do very soon—I hope you'll receive it this Week—The Box think I inform'd you in my last was traced to Colo Hoopers Parlour at Easton—from which place Carelessness, or something perhaps worse has remov'd it. So that I am apprehensive it is finally lost to the proper Owners—The Genn is determin'd to have the matter more fully enquir'd into, [th]is he's certify'd on Oath to the foregoing—Viz, his leaving the Box at Hoopers—

I am sorry Mr Dana forgot to show the Returns sooner as I was in hope they were nearly compleated before this time—I was so much hurried, that I had'nt time to take Copies of them—Neither did I keep a Copy of the Letter I sent Mr Dana, in which I specify'd the No of Returns, and the Reims of paper necessary to print them upon, supposing the printer to strike off the same Number of each kind, on the same Quantity of paper, as I have done—Your Observations upon the Necessity of some Alterations being made on account of the new Arraingment, are just. And should esteem it a very particular Favor, if you would make such as you think necessary, if your multiplicity of Business would permit—If you would be so good as to ask Mr Dana for the Letter I sent him with the Forms, you could see at once the Quantity of Paper, I found necessary upon Calculation for each sord—The whole I think amounted to 40 odd Reims—A large Quantity—But for a large Army—At least an Army that makes as many Returns necessary, as twice the N^o of Men need by reason of the smalness of our Reg^{ts}—And long Experience has shown you & me that unless printed Forms are deliver'd for the several Returns, Uniformity will never take place—Besides, I think printed Blanks, would save as much paper—as they could not be appropriated to any other purpose—Whereas blank paper is often sandalously, & fraudulently misapplied—Should esteem it as a particular Favor if you would urge on the Completion of Y^e Returns as soon as possible—If Mr Dana has'nt got the Letter by him I will send you a New Calculation—

I receiv'd the printed G Order, vs plundering—But find all Orders ineffectual to prevent it on the Lines. Even some poor Deserters from the Enemy have suffer'd plundering. All Efforts to discover the Villains have prov'd ineffectual—And I am induc'd to think there are a No of Robbers (who do not belong to either Army) that plunder and robb all without Distinction—

I wrote in my Letter to Mr Peters perhaps you hav'nt open'd it, concerning the necessary Assistance requir'd in this Office—I have two young Gentlemen with me from the Line, at present, but as there has been no fix'd Allowance for them ascertaind by Congress, I shall not be able to keep them with me much Longer—As they are exceeding closely confind. Their Duty is a Tour of mere Fatigue—More especially as I have been in a very poor State of Health this Spring (Tho much better at present)—As the Confinement is close, and by the same Rotation of Business renderd disagreeable—I shall never be able to keep Gentlemen of Honor, & Capacity in the Office—Unless They are allow'd something Handsome—As Assistants to the Adj^t. G^l were allow'd Lt Col^{os} Pay & Rations in Y^e Year of 76—I have given them Encouragement to receive the same. I wish the same may be fix'd upon by the Committee of Arraingment, & receive the Sanctions of Congress—It is needless to add to a Gentlemen so perfectly acquainted with the Duty as you are Only to request you would speak to the Committee of Arraingment in favor of my Motion And likewise with respect to the pay and Ration allow'd me—After purchasing an Horse &c &c to equip me for the Office, I find a Twelvemonth pay gone entirely—My Rations allow'd will not support my Table, Though I ever live as frugal as possible, For you must be sensible that I am inevitably expos'd to Company—So that I have a pretty disagreble prospect of undergoing the Fatigues of the Office, and at the end of the Campaign—Be involv'd in Debt—In all other Branches of the Staff Department—The most ample provisions are made—though expos'd to very little Fatigue—I wish for no unnecessary additional Expence to be added to the publick Bills—I wish for nothing extraordinary—All I want is to receive such an Allowance as may bring both Ends of the Year to Touch. If a Convenient Opportunity presented, wish you would converse with the Committee on the Subject—As I said nothing to them whilst they were at Camp—Being then too much unacquainted with the Expence, & Assistance necessarily requisite, or contingent to Y^e Office, to form any Estimate—The Enemy seem to be evacuating the City—But as they talk so openly upon the Subject, & have been so long about it; I am apt to conclude it is all fictitious, & that they will endeavor to keep the City as long as possible. However, The Majority of Voices are against me—Great part of their Troops Baggage &c are embark'd, or on the Jersey Shore—Our prisoners are put on Shipboard as I am informd'd—pray write every Opportunity to Y^r Friend & very Humble $Serv^t$.

Source: Timothy Pickering Papers, Massachusetts Historical Society.
As Adjutant General, Scammell was responsible for the Army's paperwork, which he believed was a disagreeable and unrewarding position.

Clement Biddle to Moore Furman

Dr Sir   Camp Valley Forge June 15, 1778
     I have your favour by Major Gordon & Mr Furman Yard—In answer to the last part of which first—I had Intelligence of the Oats & then of the Bags at Batsto both which I was so anxious to secure & the Owner of the privateer coming up pressing for the money I sent in three Sum to Col^o. Lawrence & Mr Ball 14.400 Ds & immediately advised you thereof for your Government—The anxiety to secure this

Cargo led me out of the regular Line but they are to Account to you—M^r. M^c.Caskey is to account & make returns as well as receive Directions from you—in short all persons Acting as Forage Masters to Cavalry or Detachments are in my Absence to receive & obey your Directions in your District—

I much approve your insisting on regular returns & accounts and of your removing all such persons as neglect Complying with your Orders therein or who meet your Disapprobation from Any other Cause—

My Letter of the 11th: answered a great part of your last but it had not reached you when Major Gordon left you—

I send you by M^r. Furman Yard the sum total for which to tell you the Truth is all I have left but a few sheets to serve me for small debts to day but we expect more Money & to have a share you may rely on—

I am clear in my Opinion that the Enemy will leave the City and in a very few Days—there ships are yet below Wilmington except a few—Not one Circumstance leads me to alter my Opinion Already given & that they mean to pass through Jersey—If we remove to the North River & I believe we shall All the forage that can be drawn from Bergen will be wanted and as few of the Farmers have thrashed their Grain there would it not be proper to apply to your Legislature to pass an Act to Oblige them to thresh the Grain & supply the Demands for the Army in such way as will least Distress them & ensure us a supply which I am afraid we shall be much short of on the North river

It is a pleasing reflection that we are so well supplied if we March through Jersey & I hope the Inhabitants will feel as little Distress as possible from an Army passing through their Country—I must see you as we go through—I am D^r sir Y^r Mo Ob^t. & Very hum serv.

Have sent Eleven Thousand Doll^s. 6000 Bills 5000 Loan Office Notes

Source: RG: Department of Defense, Subgroup: Revolutionary War, Mss. 4675, Division of Archives and Records Management, New Jersey State Archives.

Charles Lee to George Washington

Dr General,   Camp June ye 15th 1778.

As your time must necessarily be taken up by more and a greater variety of busyness than perhaps ever was impos'd on the Shoulders of any one Mortal, the most clear simple and agreeable method of communicating my sentiments on any matter of importance must certainly be by throwing em on paper—You will have more leisure to weigh and consider the strength or weakness of my arguments—and I flatter myself that what I now, or, I hope, shall at any time, offer will not be imputed to presumption impertinence or a spirit of criticism, but to my zeal for the public service. You will pardon me then when I express freely my thoughts on the present arrangement with respect to the command of the General Officers, which I cannot help thinking not only extremely defective—but that it may be productive of the worst consequences—We are, it seems, to have the superintendance of one division in the present situation of affairs, (that is as long as We remain tranquil and undisturb'd), but the instant our tranquility is disturb'd and a movement is to be made, We are to quit this division and abruptly to take the command of another—by these means, We are put out of all possibility of becoming acquainted with the names faces and characters of the officers who are to execute the orders We give, and the Soldiers who are to look up to us in the hour of tryal must be strangers to our voices and persons—They cannot consequently have that confidence in us which is so necessary and which habit and acquaintance usually inspire—indeed it appears to me not only repugnant to the rules of war, but of common prudence to introduce, for the first time, a General to his Officers and Soldiers, in the moment of attack.—I must intreat your pardon, therefore, in urging the expediency of affixing without loss of time, the respective Generals to the wings or divisions which They are to command in real actions, so that the Commanders and Commanded may not fall into the mistakes, blunders and distractions which otherwise from their being Strangers to each other must inevitably ensue—

Yesterday and the day before I had some conversation with Mr Budenot—He is from many circumstances fully persuaded that it is not the Enemy's intention to pass through the Jerseys to N. York—I have myself from the beginning been inclined to the same opinion—and on the supposition that this is not their design We ought to consider with ourselves what They most probably will do—my opinion is, that (if they are in a capacity to act offensively) They will either immediately from Philadelphia or by a feint in descending the River as far as New Castle, and then turning to the right march directly and rapidly towards Lancaster, by which means They will draw us out of our present position and oblige us to fight on terms perhaps very disadvantageous—or that They will leave Lancaster and this Army wide on the right, endeavour to take Post on the lower parts of the Susquehanna, and by securing a communication with their Ships sent round into the Bay for this purpose, be furnishd with the means of encouraging and feeding the Indian War broke out on the Western Frontier—this last plan I mention as a possibility but as less probable than the former—

If They are not in a capacity to act offensively, but are still determined to keep footing on the Continent, there are strong reasons to think that They will not shut themselves up in Towns, but take possession of some tract of Country which will afford em elbow room and sustenance, and which is so situated as to be the most effectually protected by their command of the Waters—and I have particular reasons to think that They have cast their eyes for this purpose, on the lower Counties of Delawar and some of the Maryland Counties of the Eastern Shore—that They had thoughts of adopting this measure some time ago I learnt from Mr Willin When They entertaind an idea of offering or assenting to, if proposed, a cessation of hostilities—as to any apprehensions from the unwholesomeness of ye climate They laugh at it—if They are resolv'd on this plan it certainly will be very difficult to prevent 'em or remove em afterwards as their Shipping will give em such mighty advantages. Whether They do or do not adopt any one of these plans there can be no inconvenience arise from considering the subject, nor from devising means of defeating their purposes on the supposition that They will—in short I think it woud be proper to put these queries to ourselves, shou'd They march directly towards Lancaster and the Susquehanna or indirectly from N. Castle, what are We to do? shou'd They (tho it is less probable) leave this Army and even Lancaster wide on the right, and endeavour to establish themselves on the lower parts of the Susquehanna, what are We to do? and shoud they act only on the defensive and attempt to secure to themselves some such tract of country as I have mentiond what measures are We to pursue? these are matters, I really think worthy of consideration—We have many and, I believe, able Field

Engineers in the Camp or at York; why cannot They be employ'd in some essentials, in surveying well the Country on both sides the Susquehanna—determining on the most proper Fords for our army if on any occasion They shou'd be obligd to ford it, in examining well all the best positions which may be taken betwixt the head of Elk and the Delawar, as, also betwixt Philadelphia Wilmington and Lancaster—what use may be made of Conestoga Creek if We are obligd to cover Lancaster—and (to extend their task further) how Baltimore may be put in a more defensive—state and what passes and defiles there are in one line of direction from Baltimore to York—and in another line from the part of the lower Susquehanna, where it is most probable the Enemy wou'd chuse for their landing place, to York—but I am swelling out my paper to a most insufferable bulk—and intreat Dr General that You will excuse not only it's length but whatever You find ill-tim'd or impertinent in the contents as I am, most sincerely and devotedly, Yours

P.S. Mr. Welford tells me that the Officers at Philadelphia publickly express their surprise at their General's stupidity in not marching strait to Lancaster which They say must indubitably force us out of our present position, or cover us with disgrace by laying waste the finest part of America under our noses—this evidences still stronger the necessity of examining well and immediately Conestoga Creek—where, if I am not mistaken, a fine position may be taken—He says their Cavalry now amounts to 2500 Men—that the bulk of their Force is still at Philadelphia.

Source: George Washington Papers, Roll 50, Library of Congress.

John Cadwalader to George Washington

Sir   Head Quarters 18th June 1778
    When I consider the Strength & Situation of the Enemy at Philadelphia (from the Representation made by your Excellency) I cannot think that any Enterprize can be undertaken with the least prospect of Success The distance this Army is from the City puts it out of our power to effect a Surprize—they would certainly have notice of our approach—the Troops they have in the City are, no doubt, sufficient to defend the Lines (the only point on which an Attack can be made) till a Reinforcement can re-cross the River—

It appears to me an object highly worthy the attention of this Army to annoy the Enemy on their Retreat thro' Jersey; and it is therefore absolutely necessary that the Army should immediately move from its present Situation, to some post near Delaware, & every preparation made to throw it over the River with the utmost Expedition if necessary—If the Army should remain in its present Situation till the City is evacuated, it appears to me impossible ever to overtake the Enemy; as the Troops now in Jersey are not sufficient to retard their march to Amboy, the march being easily performed in three Days—By taking post near Newtown a Division or two may be safely detached to the Banks of Delaware near Trenton, with orders to cross upon the first notice of the enemy's March—If this Disposition should enduce the Enemy to alter theirs, & to move towards our Army on this Side of Delaware, we shall have timely notice of their re-crossing the River & the Detachment as well as the Troops in Jersey may be soon brought to our Assistance—

If the Army remains in its present Situation I cannot think such a Detachment can be safely sent to Jersey as will to able, with the Troops now there, to make a serious attack upon the Enemy—And we have found from Experience that small Bodies can give very little Annoyance to an Army un-incumbered with Baggage & marching in a Line of Battle—

The first part of the fourth Questions seems to be involved in the second Question! The latter part of this Question is certainly very important; but I cannot conceive that taking possession of the Posts on the N. River to keep open a Communication with the eastern & southern States ought to be the immediate Object of this Army—As there can hardly be a doubt of the enemy's Intention to march thro' N. Jersey, I am clearly of opinion that this Army which is formidable in numbers, well equipped & well Disciplined should march immediately in full force, & in conjunction with the Troops in N Jersey, endeavour to make an effectual Stroke at the Enemy—The Situation of the Country, the position of the Enemy, the time & many other Circumstances relating to them; as well as those that relate to us, make it, in my opinion, very difficult to determine, till the Case happens, whether an Attack should be partial or general. The present, appears of me to be as good an opportunity as we shall probably have during this Contest to strike a decisive Blow—The Enemy are inferior in numbers & only prepared for a short March—If this Army should make an unfortunate Attack the Enemy could not improve their advantage, as they would find it very difficult, if not impracticable, to subsist their Army if they penetrate far into the Country—Even a Victory. if not ruinous, might in their present Situation, prove very injurious—when we consider their Strength & without any Expectation of Reinforcements; & when we consider the Situation of their affairs in Europe—

After considering all Circumstances relating to the War in America—the most important of which are, the great Reduction of their Force by frequent Actions, Defeats, Desertions, Captures & other Casualties; the immense Sum of money already expended, the little Territory acquired after three years war; the Idea of Conquest extinguished even in the minds of the Ministry; the fall of Stocks & the injury done in other respects to public Credit; the difficulty raising Troops throughout the Kingdom; the American War very unpopular in England & Ireland, & lastly the acknowledgement of the Independence of these united States by France & the Treaty entered into with that Nation—I am enduced to believe, I say, from all these Circumstances that their whole Force now in America will be drawn from these United States for the Defence of Canada, their W. India Islands & their Dominions nearer Home—Possessed of this Opinion it appears to me we have every thing to hope & nothing to fear—A Defeat of our Army will be no essential disadvantage to us & cannot in the least serve their Cause. But if this Representation of Circumstances should not have so much weight with your Excellency & you should be of opinion that the Enemy intend an Expedition on the N River I cannot think we ought to loose the present Opportunity of making an attack on the Enemy—If they are suffered, un-molested, to collect their whole Force at N York (which by your Excellency's Representation with be equal, if not superior to ours) I conceive they will have a great advantage over us by drawing their whole Force to one point; assisted too by their Fleet which will give them the Command of the Navigation; whilst our Force may be divided by the necessary Attention to a Variety of Objects—I am, Sir, with the greatest respect & esteem, your Excellency's most ob^d & very hble Servant &c

Source: George Washington Papers, Roll 50, Library of Congress.
Cadwalader was a Brigadier General of the Pennsylvania Militia. He and Enoch Poor in the following letter, were responding to Washington's request for his General's opinions, after he had laid out his observations on the enemy's current strength and possible intentions.

Enoch Poor to George Washington

Sir,   June 18th 1778

The Strength of the works at Philadelphia and the number of the Enemy are Such that I see no probability of Success if an Enterprize Should be attempted, therefore do not advise to it—should the Enemy leave Philadelphia and take their Rout to New York through Jersy I dont think it will be in the power of any Detachment you Can Send with Safety to this Camp, to give them any very considerable annoyance, and I think to move your whole army will be leaving this part of the Country togather with the Sick and the stores of the army equally exposed with the Jersies in Case you remain here—Besides Should you move into Jersy with your whole Force I have no doubt but it will bring on a General Action, which I think in our present Scituation ought to be avoided as our strength is and will be Daily increasing both in Numbers and Discipline—I am therefore full in Opinion, that we ought to Remain here until the Enemy leave Philadelphia. I am Sir your Very Hu^l. Servt

Source: George Washington Papers, Roll 50, Library of Congress.

Richard Peters to Timothy Pickering

My Dear Sir   Head Quarters June 18th. 1778

I am just setting off for Philadelphia which the Enemy evacuated this Morning immediately after Sunrise. Their Shipping appeared at 5 OClock at the Mouth of Schuylkill waiting for the Ebb. The Main Body were encamped this Morning about Billingsport. Their Light Troops were left in the City until the last, & embarked to the Number of about 3,000 on Board Transports. They have a vast Body of Horse having mounted great Numbers of their Foot on impressed Horses & they have swept the City of Saddles & Bridles. They are said to be able to fight four thousand Horse. Maxwell is in Jersey with his Brigade & a Number of Militia—but as he is not able to check them he should be cautious of falling in their Way.

I am anxious to return to York whether I was on my Way but meeting Mrs Peters on the road who was obliged to stay for some time with her Mother I returned to Camp & you may be sure I cannot resist the Opportunity of getting into Philadelphia where my Stay shall be as short as possible; but I have Property there & in its Vicinity which will demand some Attention & retard my Return, but if I can put my Business into the Hands of any one I can confide in I will not stay.

Is it not best to stop the Carpenters at the Susquehanna & the Engineers & Surveyors who are taking Drafts of that River & the Creeks?

Much Speculation is sported at Camp concerning the Hesitation or Delay of Congress on the Subject of the Commissioners Dispatches. For my part knowing the Tardiness of Proceedings I am under no Uneasiness as I am sure they are only disputing about Terms. Remember me dutifully to my Mother & accept the sincere Regards of D[r] Sir Your aff[te] Hble Serv.

I take M[rs] Peters on my Way on my return.

Source: Timothy Pickering Papers, Massachusetts Historical Society.

Philip Cortlandt to George Washington

Dear General   Valley Forge June 28th 1778
     This by Lieu[t]: Arthur Lind I send to the Adju[t]: General with a return of the Sick left in Camp when the Army march'd, have not Rec[d] the Returns from the Yellow Springs or should have sent them also Major Grier informd me that he found upon his Arrival but two Officers to Assist him in Makeing out the Returns & applyd to me for one to each Hospital which I have orderd—
I have sent One Hundred Men properly Officerd to Philad[a] by order of Major Gen[l] Arnold and have sent to the Army near 450 Men and by the latter end of the Week upwards of Five Hundred more will be ready to March which I shall send off as soon as Possible, all the Bad Cases are removd to Hospitals. Doctor Hutchinson has been most Indefatigable in procureing Waggons and Sending off the Sick—
When the Army moved there was not one Waggon left and it was some Days before the Publick Stores were Collected I had Guards placed and orderd the Officers to stop Persons from plundering & to press the Waggons that Came for that Purpose & oblige them to take the Sick to Hospitals by which means we were furnish'd with Several Good Waggons which have since been released, I could mention many Circumstances That have happened Since your Excellencys

many Circumstances That have happened Since your Excellencys
Departure which I shall omit at this time being assured that Business
of greater Importance must Engross most of your Time must therefore
beg your Excellency to Accept of my hearty well wishes for your
safety and Success hopeing that it may soon please your Excellency to
have him relieved who begs to Subscribe himself with all respect Y^r
most Obed^t Hum^l: Servt

Source: George Washington Papers, Roll 50, Library of Congress.
Cortlandt was Colonel of the Second New York Regiment. He had stayed at Valley
Forge, in charge of the 3,000 or so men who had been left behind sick. His letter
indicates he was actively sending men on to the Army as they recovered, and
safeguarding the considerable stores that remained at Valley Forge.

Document Chronology

Jedediah Huntington to Jeremiah Wadsworth, December 21, 1777.
Enoch Poor to the President of Congress, December 22, 1777.
Henry Beekman Livingston to Robert R. Livingston, December 24, 1777.
Tench Tilghman to Lord Stirling, December 25, 1777.
Benjamin Flower to Thomas Wharton Jr., December 26, 1777.
John Laurens to Henry E. Lutterloh, December 27, 1777.
Henry Knox to Sebastian Bauman, December 28, 1777.
Anthony Wayne to Thomas Wharton Jr., December 28, 1777.
Jedediah Huntington to Jabez Huntington, December 29, 1777.
Richard Platt to Alexander McDougall, December 29, 1777.
George Weedon to George Washington, December 29, 1777.
Henry E. Lutterloh to Ozias Bingham and Deputy Quarter
        Master Generals in New England, January 1, 1778.
James Mitchell Varnum to Nicholas Cooke, January 3, 1778.
Robert Ballard to Timothy Pickering, January 6, 1778.
Lachlan McIntosh, Henry Knox, William Maxwell, Enoch Poor,
        George Weedon, Jedediah Huntington, Charles Scott, John
        Paterson, and James Mitchell Varnum to Congress,
        January 6, 1778.
John Crane to Eleazer Wheelock, January 6, 1778.
Elias Boudinot to Thomas Wharton Jr., January 7, 1778.
Jedediah Huntington to Jabez Huntington, January 7, 1778.
Henry Knox to Ebenezer Stevens, January 7, 1778.
Jedediah Huntington to Jonathan Trumbull, January 9, 1778.
John Chaloner to John Ladd Howell, January 12, 1778.
Henry E. Lutterloh to John Laurens, January 15, 1778.
Clement Biddle to Timothy Matlack, January 18, 1778.
Israel Shreve to Mary Shreve, January 19, 1778.
John Crane to Eleazer Wheelock, January 21, 1778.
George Fleming to Sebastian Bauman, January 21, 1778.
Henry B. Livingston to George Washington, January 22, 1778.
William Gifford to Benjamin Holme, January 24, 1778.
Richard Platt to Alexander McDougall, January 24, 1778.
Clement Biddle to George Washington, January 25, 1778.
John Laurens to Francois Louis de Fleury, January 25, 1778.

Joseph Ward to Samuel Adams, January 26, 1778.
William Bradford Jr. to Joshua Wallace, January 27, 1778.
Gustavus B. Wallace to Michael Wallace, January 27, 1778.
Thomas Bradford to Elias Boudinot, January 28, 1778.
John Fitzgerald to Walter Stewart, January 29, 1778.
Jedediah Huntington to Joseph Trumbull, January 31 and
      February 4, 1778.
George Weedon to William Palfrey, January 31, 1778.
Alexander Scammell to Timothy Pickering, February 7, 1778.
Joseph Ward to Richard Varick, February 9, 1778.
Ephraim Blaine to John Ladd Howell, February 10, 1778.
Gustavus B. Wallace to Michael Wallace, February 13, 1778.
Thomas Jones to Charles Stewart, February 16, 1778.
Alexander Scammell to Timothy Pickering, February 19, 1778.
Hardy Murfree to Francis Lewis and John Pess with Deposition,
      February 20, 1778.
Walter Stewart to Thomas Wharton Jr., February 21, 1778.
Louis Duportail to George Washington, February 23, 1778.
Jedediah Huntington to Andrew Huntington, February 23, 1778.
Samuel Carlton to Timothy Pickering, February 24, 1778.
Charles Scott to Allen McLane, February 25, 1778.
John Chaloner to Clement Biddle, February 26, 1778.
Robert Forsyth to Timothy Pickering, February 28, 1778.
Elias Boudinot to George Washington, March 2, 1778.
Israel Shreve to Mary Shreve, March 3, 1778.
James Bradford to Thomas Wooster, March 4 and 10, 1778.
John Else to Samuel Gray, March 4, 1778.
Enoch Poor to Meshech Weare, March 4, 1778.
Jedediah Huntington to Jeremiah Wadsworth, March 5, 1778,
Ezekiel Sanford to George Washington, with an endorsement
      by Jedediah Huntington, March 7, 1778.
James Mitchell Varnum to Nathan Miller, March 7, 1778.
Israel Angell to James Mitchell Varnum, with an endorsement by
      Varnum to George Washington, March 8, 1778.
John Chaloner to John Ladd Howell, March 9, 1778.
Extract from a Letter of a Gentleman, March 9, 1778.
David Kilgore to George Washington, with an endorsement by
      Daniel Brodhead, March 10, 1778.
Jedediah Huntington to Jabez Huntington, March 13, 1778.

William Russell to Congress, March 13, 1778.
Richard Kidder Meade to Lott Brewster, March 14, 1778.
Elias Boudinot to Elisha Boudinot, March 15, 1778.
William Bradford Jr. to Tacy Wallace, March 15, 1778.
John Chaloner to Henry Champion, March 17, 1778.
Robert Hanson Harrison to Elias Boudinot, March 17, 1778.
Alexander Scammell to Timothy Pickering, March 17, 1778.
Benjamin Tupper to Henry Laurens, March 17, 1778.
David Grier to William McPherson, March 20, 1778.
Elias Boudinot to Elisha Boudinot, March 21, 1778.
Friedrich Wilhelm Augustus von Steuben Steuben to
        Horatio Gates, March 21, 1778.
Elias Boudinot to Elizabeth Ferguson, March 24, 1778.
Henry Beekman Livingston to Robert R. Livingston,
        March 25 and 27, 1778.
Richard Butler to Thomas Wharton Jr., March 26, 1778.
John Cochran to The Committee of Congress at Camp, March 26, 1778.
George Fleming to Sebastian Bauman, March 26, 1778.
Elias Boudinot to Hannah Boudinot, March 27, 1778.
Israel Angell to Luke Griffith, March 30, 1778.
Richard Platt to Timothy Pickering, March 31, 1778.
Clement Biddle to Moore Furman, April 1, 1778.
Joseph Holt to George Washington, April 1, 1778.
John Chaloner to Henry Champion, April 2, 1778.
Elias Boudinot to Horatio Gates, April 4, 1778.
John Francis Vachy to John Lamb, April 6, 1778
Alexander Scammell to John Sullivan, April 8, 1778.
James Mitchell Varnum to George Washington, April 8, 1778.
Thomas Bradford to Elias Boudinot, April 11, 1778.
Thomas Craig to Thomas Wharton Jr., April 12, 1778.
Henry Lee Jr. to Henry Laurens, April 15, 1778.
John Laurance to Timothy Pickering, April 17, 1778.
William Bradford Jr. to Tacy Wallace, April 21, 1778.
Samuel Carlton to Timothy Pickering, April 22, 1778.
Baxter How to Sebastian Bauman, April 23, 1778.
Robert Hanson Harrison to Timothy Pickering, April 23, 1778.
Clement Biddle to Moore Furman, April 25, 1778.
Anthony Wayne to William Irvine, April 27, 1778.
Ephraim Blaine to Charles Stewart, May 2, 1778.

172

Caleb North to Lord Stirling, May 2, 1778.
Clement Biddle to Moore Furman, May 5, 1778.
Charles Pettit to Moore Furman, May 5, 1778.
Lewis Farmer, Daniel Burchart, George Nagel, Christian Febiger, and
    Peter Muhlenberg to the Continental Congress. Petition for a
    German speaking chaplain, endorsed by Baron De Kalb,
    May 6, 1778.
Ephraim Blaine to Thomas Johnson, May 7, 1778.
Charles Stewart to Samuel Gray, May 10, 1778.
Henry Knox to John Lamb, May 11, 1778.
Anthony Wayne to Henry Laurens, May 13, 1778.
William Bradford Jr. to Rachel, May 14, 1778.
George Fleming to Sebastian Bauman, May 14, 1778.
Charles Pettit to Thomas Wharton, May 16, 1778.
Anthony Wayne to Henry Laurens, May 16, 1778.
John Chaloner to Jeremiah Wadsworth, May 17, 1778.
Charles Pettit to John Davis, May 17, 1778.
Clement Biddle to Moore Furman, May 18, 1778.
Richard Kidder Meade to Daniel Morgan, May 18, 1778.
Charles Pettit to Thomas Bradford, May 19, 1778.
Alexander Scammell to Allen McLane, May 20, 1778.
Clement Biddle to Thomas Wharton Jr., May 21, 1778
Anthony Wayne to Sharp Delaney, May 21, 1778.
James Craik to Jonathan Potts, May 24, 1778.
William Johnson to Allen McLane, May 24, 1778.
John Chaloner to John Ladd Howell, May 25, 1778.
Alexander Scammell to Timothy Pickering, May 26 and 27, 1778.
John Cropper to Margaret Cropper, May 29, 1778.
Tench Tilghman to James Tilghman, May 31, 1778.
Jedediah Huntington to Andrew Huntington, June 2, 1778.
Dudley Colman to Mrs. Colman, June 4, 1778.
Charles Lee to Benjamin Rush, June 4, 1778.
Jedediah Huntington to Andrew Huntington, June 5 and 7, 1778.
Eleazer Oswald to John Lamb, June 7, 1778.
Richard Peters to Timothy Pickering, June 7, 1778.
William Williams to George Washington, June 8, 1778.
Alexander Scammell to Allen McLane, June 9, 1778.
Richard Peters to Timothy Pickering, June 9, 1778.
Clement Biddle to Moore Furman, June 10, 1778.

Peter Grubb to Allen McLane, June 10, 1778.
Francis Johnston to George Washington, June 11, 1778.
Dudley Colman to Mrs. Colman, June 12, 1778.
John Conway to William Maxwell, June 12, 1778.
John Laurance to Timothy Pickering, June 13, 1778.
Alexander Scammell to Timothy Pickering, June 14, 1778.
Clement Biddle to Moore Furman? June 15, 1778.
Charles Lee to George Washington, June 15, 1778.
John Cadwalader to George Washington, June 18, 1778.
Enoch Poor to George Washington, June 18, 1778.
Richard Peters to Timothy Pickering, June 18, 1778.
Philip Cortlandt to George Washington, June 28, 1778.

INDEX